The Integrity of Elections:

The Role of Regional Organizations

The Integrity of Elections:

The Role of Regional Organizations

Contributors:
Julio Amador III
Franck Balme
Amor Boubakri
Raul Cordenillo
Andrew Ellis
Pablo Gutiérrez
Henry Ivarature
Shumbana Karume
Gillian McCormack
María Teresa Mellenkamp
Betilde Muñoz-Pogossian
Eleonora Mura
Domenico Tuccinardi

Editors:
Raul Cordenillo
Andrew Ellis

International IDEA

© International Institute for Democracy and Electoral Assistance 2012

International IDEA
Strömsborg, SE-103 34, STOCKHOLM, SWEDEN
Tel: +46 8 698 37 00, fax: +46 8 20 24 22
E-mail: info@idea.int, website: www.idea.int

The electronic version of this publication is available under a Creative Commons Licence (CCl) – Creative Commons Attribute-NonCommercial-ShareAlike 3.0 Licence. You are free to copy, distribute and transmit the publication as well as to remix and adapt it provided it is only for non-commercial purposes, that you appropriately attribute the publication, and that you distribute it under an identical license. For more information on this CCl, see: <http://creativecommons.org/licenses/by-nc-sa/3.0/>

International IDEA publications are independent of specific national or political interests. Views expressed in this publication do not necessarily represent the views of International IDEA, its Board or its Council members.

Graphic design by: Turbo Design, Ramallah
Cover photo: (Photo of the hands in the cover illustration) is taken from Corbis/Scanpix
Printed by: Trydells Tryckeri, Sweden
Design of cover: Turbo Design, Ramallah
Photo of hands on the cover: Corbis/Scanpix
ISBN: 978-91-86565-63-3

Preface

Elections can further democracy, development, human rights and security, or undermine them. For this reason, promoting and protecting the integrity of elections is critically important. Only when elections are credible can they legitimize governments, as well as effectively safeguard the right of citizens to exercise their political rights.

Regional organizations today increasingly play a role in promoting and protecting the integrity of elections. Their initiatives range from election observation to technical assistance at the national and local levels, in line with their respective mandates and the legitimacy that they draw from their member states. Their activities constitute a unique resource that needs to be harnessed.

It is therefore highly relevant that, at the inaugural meeting of the Inter-Regional Dialogue on Democracy, the heads of regional organizations agreed to focus on the integrity of elections. Launched on 15 April 2011 at the headquarters of the Organization of American States in Washington, DC, the Inter-Regional Dialogue on Democracy is a platform for engagement among regional organizations on democracy and related issues. It draws on existing cooperation between regional organizations and with International IDEA and builds on the spirit of the biennial retreat with regional organizations convened by the United Nations Secretary-General to promote inter-regional cooperation.

International IDEA, as the facilitator of the Inter-Regional Dialogue on Democracy, endeavours through this publication to capture and take stock of the experiences of regional organizations in promoting and protecting the integrity of elections. The chapters, which are organized by region, seek to increase the understanding of the roles that regional organizations play in elections in various contextually sensitive settings in their regions. They also allow for reflection on the lessons learned that could serve as food for thought for other regional organizations and democracy actors.

This publication also complements *Deepening Democracy: a Strategy for Improving the Integrity of Elections Worldwide*—the report of the Global Commission on Elections, Democracy and Security, which outlines a strategy to improve the integrity of elections worldwide. The Global Commission is a high-level panel chaired by former UN Secretary-General Kofi Annan and its recommendations highlight the role regional organizations can play in improving the integrity of elections. In particular, the Global Commission recommends that regional organizations should determine and communicate clearly their 'red lines' in relation to electoral malpractice that, if violated, would trigger multilateral condemnation and sanction. The Global Commission also recommends that regional organizations should be more proactive and engaged throughout the electoral cycle and stand up for electoral integrity before elections actually take place.

International IDEA is proud to be the facilitator of the Inter-Regional Dialogue on Democracy. I would like to express my thanks to the participating regional organizations, which have generously shared their inputs and supported this publication.

Vidar Helgesen
Secretary-General
International IDEA

Contents

Preface 5
Acronyms and abbreviations 12
Introduction 15
Raul Cordenillo and Andrew Ellis

Background 15
An overview of the chapters 17
Notes 19

1. Reflections on African Union Electoral Assistance and Observation 21
Shumbana Karume and Eleonora Mura

Introduction 21
The background to AU election observation and monitoring 22
    The OAU/AU Declaration on the
    Principles Governing Democratic Elections in Africa 25
    The African Charter on Democracy, Elections and Governance 27
    The establishment of the Democracy and Electoral Assistance Unit 29
Current AU initiatives and policy orientations 29
    From short- to long-term observation 31
    Improved coordination between the AU and the regional economic
    communities 31
    Strengthening technical and governance assistance 33
Conclusions 34
References 35
Notes 37

2. Giving ASEAN a Role in Philippine Elections: The Case for Regional Participation in Deepening Democratization Processes 41
Julio S. Amador III

Introduction	41
A brief overview of elections in the Philippines	43
The ASEAN institutional context and policies	46
ASEAN and elections	49
Laying institutional foundations	50
Conclusions	53
References and further reading	54
Notes	55

3. The Evolution of Election Observation in the European Union: From Fraud Prevention to Democracy Support ... 57
Domenico Tuccinardi, Franck Balme and Gillian McCormack

Introduction	57
The Declaration of Principles for International Election Observation	59
No longer just 'free and fair'	61
What international standards?	62
The impact on EU election observation	64
The underrated value of domestic election observation	66
Domestic observers and observation around the electoral process	68
The regional dimension of international observation	70
Conclusions	72
References	74
Notes	75

4. The League of Arab States and the Electoral Gap ... 77
Amor Boubakri

Introduction	77
The Arab League and democratization in the Arab region	79
The Arab League and elections	81
A modest involvement	81
The legal and institutional framework	82
Electoral assistance	84
The observation missions	85
The geographical focus of election observation missions	86
A focus on presidential elections	86
A trend towards collaborative action	86
The main difficulties of the Arab League's observation missions	88
A lack of means	88
A lack of guidelines	88
What role for the Arab League in future elections?	89
Conclusions	90

Selected bibliography 90
Notes 92

5. The Responsibility to Expose: The Role of OAS Electoral Observation Missions in the Promotion of the Political Rights of Women 95
Betilde Muñoz-Pogossian

Introduction 95
Making women's participation in the electoral process visible: a theoretical
    framework.. 96
Gender equality in the Americas... 97
The role of the OAS 98
The methodology at work: beyond the theoretical framework 101
    Paraguay 101
    Peru 103
    Guatemala 104
    Colombia 105
    Guyana 106
    Mainstreamed perspective in OAS EOMs: the example of Saint Lucia...... 106
Conclusions 107
References.. 111
Notes 111
    Table 5.1 Women's participation in elections in Latin America:
        a comparative overview 108
    Figure 5.1 Participation by women in OAS electoral observation missions   99
    Figure 5.2 The concept of democratic elections.. 100

6. Quality Management Systems and their Contribution to the Integrity of Elections 115
María T. Mellenkamp and Pablo Gutiérrez

Introduction 115
Quality management systems 117
    Certification under ISO quality management standards............................ 117
    Quality management principles 118
    Certification process actors 119
Promoting electoral quality.. 119
    OAS electoral technical cooperation on QMS
        and ISO standards certification... 121
    OAS methodology for the introduction of QMS
        and ISO certification for EMBs 121
Country cases 123

The Panamanian certification	123
The Peruvian certification	125
The Costa Rican certification	128
The adoption of an international electoral ISO standard	129
Conclusions	131
References and further reading	132
Notes	132
Figure 6.1 The actors involved in the QMS implementation process and certification under ISO quality standards for the Jurado Nacional de Elecciones de Perú	120
Figure 6.2 OAS Methodology stages	122
Figure 6.3 ISO-certified processes in Panama	125
Figure 6.4 Four key certified processes in Peru	126
Figure 6.5 Courses and training sessions in Peru	127
Figure 6.6 Objectives and scope of the diagnostic in Costa Rica	129
Box 6.1 The JNE quality policy	128

7. Election Observation by the Pacific Islands Forum: Experiences and Challenges 135
Henry Ivarature

Introduction	135
The Pacific Islands Forum and its Secretariat	136
A mandate to observe elections	137
The Biketawa Declaration and the three key principles	137
EOMs and the PIF Observer Group: an extension of the 'Secretary General's good offices role'	138
Domestic guidelines for international election observers	140
The PIF's endorsement of the Declaration of Principles and Code of Conduct	141
Joint EOMs: the PIF and the Commonwealth	142
Strengths and weaknesses	143
Case study 1: The Solomon Islands	143
Case study 2: The Autonomous Region of Bougainville	145
Case study 3: The Republic of Nauru	146
Prospects and recommendations	147
From the short-term to the long-term	147
Follow-up	148
Development of regional norms	149
Alternatives to election observation: meetings of EMBs	150
Recommendations on gender in EOM reports and EOMs	151
Conclusions: strengthening PIF election observation practice	151

References 153
Notes 155
    Table 7.1 Summary of EOMs and observers on Forum EOMs
        from 2001 to 2011 152

Conclusions 157
Raul Cordenillo and Andrew Ellis

Election observation missions 158
Technical assistance or cooperation 159
Gender mainstreaming 160
Domestic observation 160
Is there convergence? 160
Reflections 161
Notes 161

About the Authors 162

Acronyms and abbreviations

ANFREL	Asian Network for Free Elections
APRM	African Peer Review Mechanism
APSC	ASEAN Political-Security Community
ASCC	ASEAN Socio-Cultural Community
ASEAN	Association of Southeast Asian Nations
AU	African Union
CFSP	Common Foreign and Security Policy (European Union)
COMELEC	Commission on Elections (the Philippines)
DEAU	Democracy and Electoral Assistance Unit (of the African Union)
DECO	Department for Electoral Cooperation and Observation (Organization of American States)
EISA	Electoral Institute for Sustainable Democracy in Africa
EMB	electoral management body
ENEMO	European Network of Electoral Monitoring Organizations
EOM	election observation missions
EOP	election observation programme (Pacific Islands Forum)
FOG	Forum Observer Group (Pacific Islands Forum)
EU	European Union
FIC	Forum island countries (Pacific Islands Forum)
IOF	Organization Internationale de la Francophonie
ISO	International Organization for Standardization
JNE	Jurado Nacional de Elecciones de Perú (National Electoral Jury of Peru)
LAS	League of Arab States
NAMFREL	National Citizens' Movement for Free Elections (the Philippines)
NEEDS	Network for Enhanced Electoral and Democratic Support
NDI	National Democratic Institute for International Affairs
NEPAD	New Partnership for Africa's Development
NGO	non-governmental organization
OAS	Organization of American States
OAU	Organization of African Unity
OAV	overseas absentee voting

12 International IDEA

ODIHR	Office for Democratic Institutions and Human Rights (Organization for Security and Co-operation in Europe)
OSCE	Organization for Security and Co-operation in Europe
PIF	Pacific Islands Forum
PNG	Papua New Guinea
PVT	parallel vote tabulation
QMS	Quality Management System
REC	regional economic community
RMI	Republic of the Marshall Islands
SAARC	South Asian Association for Regional Cooperation
UN	United Nations

Introduction

Introduction

Raul Cordenillo and Andrew Ellis

Background

Regional organizations are among the key actors in present-day international relations. They foster dialogue among states and serve as a platform for the discussion of various transnational economic, political and social issues. They also play an increasingly important role in elections.

Elections are a cornerstone of democracy. They empower people to participate in the selection of their political representatives. Protecting and promoting the integrity of elections is therefore a top policy priority.

Troubled electoral processes and their fall-out have challenged the credibility of democracy in recent years. Elections that are recognized as free and fair result in a peaceful transition of power, while electoral processes that are deemed fraudulent or violent, or to have been manipulated, can either lead to or exacerbate political instability.

Ultimately, protecting and promoting the integrity of elections is the responsibility of all national stakeholders. To this end, states not only pass legislation, set up institutions or draw up codes of conduct and other enforcement mechanisms at the national level, but also commit themselves to regional and international principles of democracy. This is where regional organizations draw their respective mandates to work on elections. Their initiatives range from election observation missions (EOMs) to dialogue and cooperation on various issues with the electoral management bodies (EMBs) of their member states. Some regional organizations also provide technical assistance or cooperate on the implementation of recommendations emanating from EOMs, which seek to improve or correct specific aspects of democratic elections.

The Organization of American States (OAS) started to monitor elections in the 1960s. The African Union (AU), the European Union (EU), the League of Arab States (LAS) and the Pacific Islands Forum (PIF) are all currently undertaking EOMs. The Association of Southeast Asian Nations (ASEAN) has also begun monitoring elections and the South Asian Association for Regional Cooperation (SAARC) has undertaken EOMs in the past. In some of these regional organizations, meetings among the EMBs of their member states are held regularly and electoral technical assistance and cooperation are part and parcel of their political cooperation.

The experiences of regional organizations are a unique resource that needs to be harnessed and shared not only with their peers, but also with other democracy actors. The meeting of the Inter-Regional Dialogue on Democracy, a platform for engagement among regional organizations on democracy and related issues which was launched on 15 April 2011, agreed to focus initially on the role that regional organizations can play in promoting and protecting the integrity of elections.

This publication is a collection of background papers prepared for the Inter-Regional Workshop on Regional Organizations and the Integrity of Elections, which took place in Stockholm in December 2011. The papers, presented here as chapters, focus on the regional organizations that participate in the Inter-Regional Dialogue on Democracy.[1]

The different chapters aim to highlight the mandates and election-related initiatives of the regional organizations, including gender mainstreaming, as well as their achievements, challenges and limitations. Some are written from an insider perspective, since they are contributions from officials within the regional organizations. Others contain perspectives from observers in the respective regions. The chapters discuss policy implications and make recommendations that regional organizations and policymakers should consider and may wish to take further.

It is notable that the majority of the initiatives by regional organizations are related to EOMs. It is therefore tempting to make a binary classification of the initiatives as either EOM-related or not. Such a delineation, however, would miss the opportunity to appreciate the differences in the mandates of regional organizations, as well as the variations in the contexts in which they operate. This is easy to miss when examining regional organizations, particularly in a collection of this nature. The chapters are presented in alphabetical order by name of regional organization.

An overview of the chapters

Since the 1990s, the AU has observed close to 250 elections across a majority of its 54 member states. It has developed a framework for election observation that allows for the institutionalization of its mandate and for the increased professionalization and standardization of its procedures and methodologies. Beyond EOMs, its current initiatives extend to electoral assistance and governance support. A designated unit, the Democracy and Electoral Assistance Unit, has been established within the Political Affairs Department. Chapter 1, Reflections on African Union Electoral Assistance and Observation, captures the AU experience, highlighting in particular its policy interventions, new initiatives and future priorities.

Chapter 2, 'Giving ASEAN a Role in Philippine Elections: The Case for Regional Participation in Deepening Democratization Processes', was written prior to ASEAN's observation mission to the 1 April 2012 by-elections in Myanmar. It essentially advocates a role for ASEAN in the conduct of elections in its member states by highlighting ASEAN's commitments to deepening democracy and achieving good governance in the proposed ASEAN Community. Using the Philippines as an example of a member state in which ASEAN might play a role as an observer of the conduct of national elections, it advances the view that ASEAN could act as an intermediary for electoral praxis and technology. The mission to Myanmar may have started this process, but there is as yet no institutionalization of such practice in ASEAN.

Chapter 3, 'The Evolution of Election Observation in the European Union: From Fraud Prevention to Democracy Support', highlights the emergence of EOMs as a democracy support instrument of EU external policy. Placed in the context of the key developments in international election observation since 2000, the chapter discusses the role that EOMs play in the EU strategy for democracy promotion in the post-Lisbon Treaty setting. Recognizing the impact, as well as the limitations, of EOMs, it sets out options for further programming in the field of election observation.

Chapter 4, 'The League of Arab States and the Electoral Gap', examines the involvement of the LAS in election observation and assistance. It points out that, despite its limited mandate, as well as the absence of a specific legal framework to guide its work, the LAS has committed itself to EOMs and is gradually overcoming the challenges at hand. The chapter argues that the LAS can play an important role in election observation and assistance, and suggests a set of electoral support and observation policies that would enable the LAS to meet international standards and bolster its modest achievements to date.

As the regional organization that has been undertaking EOMs for the longest time, the OAS has rich experience of innovation, and particularly of implementing the recommendations of such EOMs. Chapter 5, 'The Responsibility to Expose: The Role of OAS Electoral Observation Missions in the Promotion of the Political Rights of Women', describes a pioneering initiative by the OAS to design a standardized methodology for incorporating a gender perspective into its election observation efforts. It argues that the incorporation of a gender perspective would allow OAS EOMs to bring issues of gender equity and women's political rights to the fore and help place these concerns on the political agenda. The chapter also identifies and exposes the barriers to the equal participation of women and men in electoral processes, and provides food for thought for policymakers and other organizations that conduct EOMs.

Chapter 6, 'Quality Management Systems and their Contribution to the Integrity of Elections', presents a new phase of cooperation between the OAS and the EMBs of its member states. This is the implementation of a Quality Management System (QMS), which ends in the certification of electoral processes or structures under International Standard ISO 9001. The chapter highlights the maturity required by EMBs to make a qualitative leap in their structure and operations, as well as the way in which they relate to their 'clients'. It concludes that this form of technical cooperation could be applicable to other organizations that carry out electoral technical assistance or cooperation.

Chapter 7, 'Election Observation by the Pacific Islands Forum: Experiences and Challenges', highlights the political features and region-specific aspects of PIF EOMs and makes policy recommendations to strengthen the PIF's election monitoring programme.

The chapters in this publication are just a cross-section of a larger group of papers prepared for the Inter-Regional Workshop. Details of the Workshop and all the papers are available on the website of the Inter-Regional Democracy Resource, the secretariat of the Inter-Regional Dialogue on Democracy.[2]

Notes

[1] The participants in the Inter-Regional Dialogue on Democracy are the AU, ASEAN, the EU, the LAS, the OAS, the PIF and SAARC with International IDEA as the facilitator. Efforts were made to obtain a paper focused on SAARC, but these were unsuccessful, largely due to the fact that SAARC does not have a direct mandate to engage in election-related initiatives. It should be noted, however, that there have been a few EOM-related initiatives by SAARC, including the deployment of non-governmental election observers to the parliamentary elections in Bangladesh, held on 12 June 1996.

[2] See <http://www.idea.int/democracydialog/workshop-on-regional-organizations.cfm>.

Chapter 1

Reflections on African Union Electoral Assistance and Observation

Chapter 1

Shumbana Karume and Eleonora Mura

Reflections on African Union Electoral Assistance and Observation

Introduction

The predecessor to the African Union (AU), the Organization of African Unity (OAU), began showing a marked interest in the promotion of democracy and the integrity of elections in Africa in the early 1990s. The involvement of the OAU was marked by the adoption of declarations and resolutions, and by its undertakings in the field of election observation and assistance.

The first of the declarations in which African heads of state and government agreed that the OAU must involve itself in the democratization process on the African continent was the Declaration of the Assembly of Heads of State and Government of the Organization of African Unity on the Political and Socio-Economic Situation in Africa and the Fundamental Changes Taking Place in the World, which was formally adopted in July 1990. At the beginning of the new millennium, the OAU and then the AU adopted numerous declarations and decisions on the promotion of democracy and good governance.[1] These include, first and foremost, the Constitutive Act of the African Union, the founding document of the AU and the first document to enshrine the promotion of democracy as part of the core mandate of the AU. Other important declarations are the Lomé Declaration of July 2000 on the Framework for an OAU response to unconstitutional changes of government, the Declaration on the Principles Governing Democratic Elections in Africa (the Durban Declaration) of 2002 and the African Charter on Democracy, Elections and Governance (May 2007).

All these legal instruments confirm the commitment of the AU not only to the integrity of elections, but also to the overall strengthening of democratic institutions and good governance in Africa. These legal instruments are the foundation for the comprehensive legal and institutional framework for the AU's action in the field of democracy building.

This chapter provides a holistic overview of the work of the AU in the field of democratization, focusing in particular on election observation and electoral assistance. It describes the evolution of the legal and institutional framework for the AU's work in the field of democratization, and reflects on recent AU initiatives and policy orientations.

The background to AU election observation and monitoring

Election observation emerged as a significant mechanism for supporting democratic development in the post-Cold War period. The 1989 elections in Sandinista Nicaragua and the referendum on self-determination in Namibia were early examples. On both occasions, the United Nations (UN) deployed observers jointly with regional organizations to report on the democratic quality of electoral practices.[2]

The OAU's first involvement in election observation was in 1989, when it joined the UN in monitoring elections in Namibia to ensure the fulfilment of United Nations Security Council Resolution 435 (1978), to oversee an internationally agreed decolonization plan for Namibia.

In 1990, the majority of African countries were one-party states. A combination of the end of the Cold War and increasing domestic demand for political reform triggered a process of transition to democracy in many African countries, and therefore multiparty and recurrent elections.

It was in this context that most African countries turned to the OAU for assistance. In response, the OAU Secretary General, Salim Ahmed Salim, stressed that it was the duty and responsibility of the OAU to respond positively and effectively to appeals from its constituent members to assist in the democratic transitions, in particular through election observation. He also stressed the need to build the capacity of the OAU Secretariat to deal with electoral observation.[3]

Until the end of the 1980s, the OAU had adhered strictly to the principle of non-interference in the internal affairs of its member states, which had been enshrined in Article 3 of the Charter of the OAU. The governance focus of the OAU 'was on the elimination of the last vestiges of colonialism in order to promote the principle of self-determination and to foster the establishment of truly sovereign states, free from all forms of external interference'.[4] This strong respect for the non-interference principle has to be understood from a historical perspective and in the context of decolonization.

Its involvement in election observation began a new era for the OAU and its role in the democratization of the African continent. Secretary General Salim Ahmed Salim expressed this new attitude on several occasions, confirming that the OAU would now play a role in democratization.[5] The OAU soon began to undertake election observation missions independently, and its interest in election observation developed hand in hand with its growing involvement in the democratization of Africa. It was with the Declaration on the Political and Socio-Economic Situation in Africa and the Fundamental Changes Taking Place in the World that the OAU officially engaged with the democratization process on the African continent.[6]

Towards the end of the 1990s, the OAU recognized the importance of democratization processes in Africa, formally condemning changes of government which violated the constitution of the relevant country. In 1999, during its 35th Ordinary Session of the Assembly of Heads of State and Government, in Algiers, the OAU took a tougher stance and strengthened the measures against unconstitutional changes in power (the Algiers Declaration, July 1999). On this occasion, the Assembly of the OAU adopted two decisions on the issue: the first concerned the imposition of sanctions on governments that came to power through unconstitutional means; and the second called on the OAU Secretary General to assist countries intending to return to constitutional rule and monitor their progress after the constitutional order was restored. Following up on the Algiers Declaration, as is noted above, in July 2000, the Assembly of Heads of State and Government adopted the Lomé Declaration on the Framework for an OAU response to unconstitutional changes of government. The Lomé Declaration was an important step forward in the formulation by the OAU of a global approach to the problem of unconstitutional changes of government. It was structured around four elements: a set of common values and principles for democratic governance; a common definition of what constitutes unconstitutional change; measures and actions that the OAU could progressively take to respond to an unconstitutional change; and an implementation mechanism.

The Lomé Declaration provided an additional stimulus for the OAU's agenda on the democratization process. It provided a framework of punitive measures, such as limited and targeted sanctions, that could be taken by the OAU in the event that, after a period of six months from the initial condemnation of the unconstitutional change, the perpetrators of such a change refused to restore the constitutional order (Tazorora 2008). It is evident that OAU attitudes to democracy, human rights and good governance had become more forthright. These developments prepared the ground for issues of governance, democracy and human rights to become the centrepiece of the agenda of the emergent AU.

The AU Constitutive Act was the first document of the new AU era to declare that the AU 'shall promote democratic principles and institutions'. The Preamble to the Constitutive Act specifies the determination of member states 'to promote and protect human and peoples' rights, consolidate democratic institutions and culture, and to ensure good governance and the rule of law'.

Articles 3 and 4 of the Constitutive Act codify the promotion of 'democratic principles and institutions, popular participation and good governance' and 'the right of the Union to intervene in a Member State pursuant to a decision of the Assembly in respect of grave circumstances, namely: war crimes, genocide and crimes against humanity', respectively. Article 4 thus gives the AU unprecedented powers of intervention: a true watershed moment marking the end of the absolute dominance of the principle of non-interference.

Article 30 of the Constitutive Act unambiguously enshrines a categorical rejection by the AU of unconstitutional changes of government. Article 30 stipulates that 'Governments which shall come to power through unconstitutional means shall not be allowed to participate in the activities of the Union'.

While describing the legal background shaping the framework for the AU's work in the field of electoral observation, it is important to mention several policy documents that do not directly address electoral observation and assistance, but have contributed to shaping the work of the AU in the field of democratization. In particular, it is worth mentioning the New Partnership for Africa's Development (NEPAD 2001) and specifically NEPAD's Democracy and Political Governance Initiative, which saw African leaders commit themselves to promote and protect democracy and human rights in their respective countries and regions by developing clear standards of accountability and participatory governance at the national and sub-regional levels. In this respect, NEPAD is more of an economic development strategy: the partnership puts unprecedented emphasis on democracy and good governance in African strategies and programmes, establishing democratic governance as crucial for socio-economic development. Furthermore, another landmark African document, the African Charter on Human and Peoples'

Rights, adopted in Nairobi in June 1981, recognizes the right of every citizen to participate freely in the government of his or her country either directly or through democratically elected representatives.

Two additional documents must be cited in this review: the African Charter for Popular Participation in Development, adopted in Addis Ababa in July 1990, which emphasizes the need to involve the people of Africa in the spheres of economic and political governance; and the Cairo Agenda for Action, adopted in Cairo in 1995, which stresses the imperative of ensuring democratic governance through popular participation based on respect for human rights and dignity, free and fair elections, and respect for the principles of freedom of the press, free speech, and freedom of association and conscience.

However, the milestones for AU work in the field of democratization are the OAU/AU Declaration on the Principles Governing Democratic Elections in Africa, also known as the Durban Declaration, and the African Charter on Democracy, Elections and Governance. These two documents allow the AU to be fully engaged in election observation and in the strengthening of election processes. Together, all these documents form the foundations for the work of the AU in the field of democratization.

The OAU/AU Declaration on the Principles Governing Democratic Elections in Africa

The OAU/AU Declaration on the Principles Governing Democratic Elections in Africa or Durban Declaration, which was endorsed at the 38th Ordinary Session of the OAU Assembly, is the foundation on which the AU has sought to drive the development of democratic election processes across the continent. It embraces fully the principle that democratic elections are the sole legitimate basis for authority for a representative government, and cites the holding of regular elections as an important tool for conflict prevention, conflict management and conflict resolution.

The Durban Declaration lists the responsibilities of the OAU/AU member states to: (a) take measures to implement the principles contained in it; (b) establish, where they are lacking, appropriate institutions to decide on issues such as codes of conduct, citizenship requirements, residency requirements, age requirements for eligible voters and the compilation of electoral registers; (c) establish impartial, inclusive, competent and accountable national electoral management bodies (EMBs) staffed with qualified personnel, as well as competent legal entities, including effective constitutional courts, with authority of arbitration in the event of disputes arising from the conduct of elections; and (d) safeguard the human and civil liberties of all citizens, including the freedom of movement, assembly, association, expression and to campaign, as well as access to the media by all stakeholders, particularly during the electoral process.

Moreover, the Durban Declaration sets out rights and principles relating to democratic elections, such as that: (a) every citizen shall have the right to participate freely in the government of his or her country, either directly or through freely elected representatives in accordance with the provisions of the law; (b) every citizen has the right to participate fully in the electoral processes of the country, including the right to vote or be voted for, according to the laws of the country and as guaranteed by the constitution, without any kind of discrimination; (c) every citizen shall have the right to free association and assembly in accordance with the law; and (d) every citizen shall have the freedom to establish or to be a member of a political party or organization in accordance with the law.

Thus, in the Durban Declaration, the heads of state and government mandate that the OAU/AU be fully engaged in strengthening the democratization process, particularly by observing elections in member states. In addition, the Durban Declaration provides strict guidelines and mandates for the OAU/AU to take all necessary measures to ensure its implementation. In particular it strengthens the role of the OAU/AU in observing elections in accordance with a memorandum of understanding reached with the country concerned, and in mobilizing extra-budgetary funds to augment the OAU/AU's resource base in order to facilitate the implementation of the Declaration.

The first rule for OAU/AU election observers is that they shall operate within the guidelines of the Commission, based on the Durban Declaration. The Commission is required to keep an up-to-date election calendar for the OAU/AU member states. According to Paragraph V of the Durban Declaration, the country holding elections should send a formal invitation to the OAU through the national electoral commission, another electoral authority or the government. The OAU, on receiving an invitation to observe an election, shall ensure that adequate lead time is available for preparation; access is secured to essential planning information; there is access to competent and relevant expertise; and there are sufficient financial and other resources to undertake election observation and related activities.

It is a key stipulation of the guidelines that on receiving an invitation to observe an election, the OAU/AU Commission should expeditiously dispatch an election assessment team to the country planning the election. The assessment team should establish whether conditions exist in the country for organizing credible, legitimate, free and fair elections in accordance with the Durban Declaration. The head of the assessment team should then advise the OAU/AU Commission accordingly.

In addition, the Durban Declaration mandates the OAU/AU to compile and maintain a roster of African experts in the field of election observation and democratization, and to avail itself of their expertise by deploying competent and professional observers whenever necessary. This provision marks the beginning of the professionalization of election observation by the African Union. To this end, the OAU/AU Secretariat must also formulate standards for procedures, preparations and the treatment of personnel selected to serve in OAU/AU observer missions.

Compared to previous commitments, the Durban Declaration provides clear and specific guidelines with regard to free and fair elections and with respect to the monitoring role of the OAU/AU. However, it must be underlined that the Declaration is still a soft law instrument that is not legally binding, and therefore the application of its provisions relies fully on the 'goodwill' of the member states.

The Durban Declaration is also important because it provided a mandate for the creation in 2006 of a dedicated Democracy and Electoral Assistance Unit within the Political Affairs Department of the OAU/AU Commission. The raison d'être for the establishment of this unit can be clearly identified in the need for the Commission to implement its programme on the advancement of democracy and democratic elections on the continent.

The African Charter on Democracy, Elections and Governance

The African Charter on Democracy, Elections and Governance is the most comprehensive commitment by the AU to deepening and consolidating democratic governance in Africa. It builds on the commitments and declarations that were cited earlier and serves as a consolidated point of reference for all AU efforts aimed at enhancing democracy, elections and governance across the continent.

Many of the policy documents that frame the mandate of the AU in the field of electoral assistance and observation are of a non-binding nature and therefore can only provide guidance. The Charter, by contrast, is a legally binding document.

Since its entry into force on 15 February 2012,[7] the Charter has set the legal framework of the AU's work on democratization. The next step for the AU will be to secure an effective commitment from the national leaderships to the principles of the Charter, including adoption of the measures needed to institutionalize good economic and corporate governance, and to incorporate the provisions of the Charter into national laws, policies and regulations. It is important to ensure that signing the Charter is seen not just as a symbolic act but as one backed by a genuine commitment.

The provisions contained in the Charter are premised on universal values of democracy, respect for human rights, the rule of law, and the supremacy of the constitution and the constitutional order in the political arrangements of AU member states. In addition, and in relation to electoral assistance, the Charter emphasizes the importance of pre-election observation, election observation missions (EOMs) and special advisory missions as well as the need to create an environment that is conducive to independent and impartial national observation mechanisms.

Among other provisions, the Charter re-addresses issues around unconstitutional changes of government, putting strong emphasis on the obligation to ensure the independence of the judiciary. With regard to electoral management, the Charter promotes best practices in the management of elections and the obligation to hold transparent, free and fair elections in accordance with the Durban Declaration. In addition, the Charter includes provisions on the strengthening of national mechanisms for redress in election disputes and a binding code of conduct for political stakeholders. The Charter also contains provisions regulating the free and equitable access by political parties to state-controlled media during elections.

Finally, the Charter devotes particular attention to the crucial role of women in the development and strengthening of democracy. Article 29 of the Charter mandates states parties to create the necessary conditions for the full and active participation of women in decision-making processes and structures at all levels as a fundamental element in the promotion and exercise of a democratic culture. In addition, Article 29 mandates states parties to take all possible measures to encourage the full and active participation of women in the electoral process and ensure gender parity in representation at all levels, including legislatures.

The establishment of the Democracy and Electoral Assistance Unit

As highlighted earlier, in July 2002 during the 38th Ordinary Session of the OAU Assembly in Durban, the OAU Council of Ministers, through the Durban Declaration, decided to establish an administrative unit to observe elections, follow up the implementation of recommendations and generally assist the Commissioner in charge of the Political Affairs Department, which was responsible, in collaboration with the official authorities of the countries concerned, for coordinating the OAU/AU's observation of elections.

Following a feasibility study and consultations with evaluations for independent and governmental experts in the field, in June 2006, the Executive Council of the AU decided to set up the Democracy and Electoral Assistance Unit (DEAU) within the Political Affairs Department of the AU Commission. The DEAU was made responsible for coordinating and implementing all AU Commission actions aimed at promoting democracy and elections in Africa. It has a broad mandate to promote democracy, observe elections and provide electoral assistance.

In addition to approving the creation of the DEAU, the Executive Council also approved the establishment of a dedicated trust fund, the Democracy and Electoral Assistance Fund, to support the activities of the DEAU. This fund is proof of the AU's concrete commitment to strengthening democratization. However, in practice the fund remains heavily dependent on international donors. In this regard it has been noted elsewhere that 'for democracy to advance and deepen, African States should be prepared to earmark resources for democratic and electoral processes' (Pretorius 2008).

Current AU initiatives and policy orientations

More than 20 years have passed since the initial engagement by the OAU in the field of democratization. In this time, African countries have made remarkable progress in instituting the core principles and practices of democratic governance. However, there is no denying that the results achieved so far have been mixed (AU 2009). The violence that has accompanied recent elections highlights the importance of further enhancing the AU's effectiveness in dealing with such situations.

Since 2002, the AU has developed a clear and effective framework for election observation that has allowed for the institutionalization of its mandate and the increased professionalization and standardization of its procedures and methodologies in matters of electoral observation. Since the 1990s, the

OAU and then the AU have observed close to 250 elections in a majority of the 54 AU member states. Building on the broad overview of the legal and institutional framework of the AU electoral observation and assistance instruments, this section discusses the work that has been implemented so far and describes recent initiatives and policy orientations undertaken by the AU.

Since 2008, following the absence of any invitation to observe the 2007 elections in Kenya, the AU has taken unprecedented steps to observe elections even when not invited. This must be acknowledged as fundamental progress in the AU's practice of election observation. The decision to observe elections without an invitation to do so from the host country must be seen as an extremely positive development as it underlines a strong commitment by the AU to be the driver of democratic change on the continent. In addition, ensuring the observation of *all* elections held by its member states reinforces the role of the AU in promoting and protecting the integrity of elections at the regional level.

AU election observation is currently regarded as a peer-pressure mechanism within Africa that can exercise powerful influence for the establishment of democratic governments. Electoral observation and assistance are tangible and visible tools for the implementation of the commitments to democratization made by the AU at its creation—commitments that distinguish it from its predecessor, which was often criticized for its weakness in monitoring human rights and good governance. Many authors have noticed how the AU took stock of the failures of the OAU and adopted an increasingly interventionist stance through its legal frameworks and institutions, moving from a non-interventionist stance to an open non-indifference approach (Mwanasali 2008). As one commentator wrote, 'until very recently, the principles of national sovereignty and non-intervention were the official norms of the OAU. In contrast, the Constitutive Act of the AU proclaimed a paradigmatic shift towards collective responsibility in matters of human and state security' (Melber 2006).

The fact that the observers nominated by the Chairperson of the African Union Commission are usually senior and respected personalities gives the AU further political leverage, particularly when it comes to the AU's EOMs. AU EOMs are often headed by former presidents of African countries. Other members of the team often include the heads of the independent electoral commissions. Finally, the AU EOMs often include members of various African civil society organizations. The mixed composition of the observer teams enhances the balance and credibility of the EOMs. The observers receive specific training on electoral observation and employ standardized methodologies. Building on these important elements, following the establishment of the DEAU, several initiatives have been implemented to further enhance the effectiveness of the work of the African Union in this field.

From short- to long-term observation

AU election observation still mainly deploys short-term missions. In many cases, observers are deployed one week before the elections and are therefore unable to observe procedures related to voter registration or to monitor the media and how political parties finance their campaigns. In this respect, the balance between short- and long-term observation has become a priority for the AU Commission. Long-term observation allows for the effective observation of all the stages of elections, that is, the pre-voting, voting and post-voting stages, demarcation of electoral boundaries, political party registration, candidate nomination, party funding, political campaigns, the role of the security forces, the use of state resources, and the media environment. Long-term observation also allows comprehensive reporting and stocktaking on how the electoral process is conducted, leading to broader learning. The AU Commission would then have a comprehensive overview at its disposal, leading to better targeting of any technical or governance assistance projects to be implemented in the member states. Furthermore, by improving the information available during the pre-election period, election monitors could have an impact on defusing post-election disputes (Beaulieu 2011).

The Political Affairs Department, through the DEAU, is implementing a road map that will allow the African Union Commission to make a paradigm shift from short- to long-term election observation based on the electoral cycle approach. This means that the AU will be able to pilot long-term election observation by the end of 2012, and later mainstream it further.

Improved coordination between the AU and the regional economic communities

One of the main challenges that regional organizations commonly face is the high financial cost of deploying EOMs. One way for the AU to counterbalance the limited availability of resources would be to enhance its collaboration with the regional economic communities (RECs). Better coordination of the election observation efforts of the AU and the RECs would enhance their effectiveness. In this regard, the establishment of the African Governance Architecture is a positive effort by the AU Commission to establish synergies and interactions between African institutions and organs with a formal governance mandate. The African Governance Architecture aims to strengthen and enhance the capacity of the AU institutions working in the field of democratic governance and to produce 'shared agendas'. In this context, the African Governance Platform was established to strengthen cooperation and coordination between different stakeholders. Effective collaboration between the AU, the RECs and other regional and national civil society organization networks will improve the effectiveness of election observation and minimize duplication of effort in the field, as well as costs, thereby helping the AU and the other actors to better channel their limited resources.

It should be emphasized that collaboration between the AU Commission and the RECs is mandated in the African Charter on Democracy, Elections and Governance. The concrete steps towards more integrated activities started with a meeting in Sudan in 2009. Further momentum was provided and the need for deeper collaboration identified at a meeting held with national EMBs in Accra in December 2009, and in numerous follow-up meetings organized to discuss the African Charter on Democracy, Elections and Governance. These meetings serve to ensure that the AU Commission and the RECs move beyond rhetoric on collaboration to enhance their impact through more effective cooperation.

Many of the uncoordinated election observation activities by the AU Commission and the RECs were a direct result of their different mandates. Not enough time was spent building modalities for working together on African elections. As election observation became more common and more rooted in continental electoral practices, the need to ensure consistency in and uniformity of election observer missions among regional and continental organizations increased.

A specific plan of action for operationalizing cooperation in the area of election observation between the AU and the RECs has yet to be developed. In the meantime, ad hoc cooperation between AU and REC observers through exchanges of information, monitoring the pre-election environment, sharing information on the dispatch of advance teams and briefing observers forms the basis for ongoing collaboration. These areas of cooperation have led to a much closer working relationship.

Strengthening technical and governance assistance

As is noted above, the DEAU has a mandate to implement all the activities defined by the AU Commission aimed at promoting democracy and democratic elections in Africa, offering electoral assistance and support to democracy in all member states. The African Charter on Democracy, Elections and Governance recognizes the role of the AU in strengthening the capacity of electoral authorities to manage elections. Article 18, Sub-section 1 of the Charter states that 'State Parties may request the Commission, through the Democracy and Electoral Assistance Unit and the Democracy and Electoral Assistance Fund, to provide advisory services or assistance for strengthening and developing their electoral institutions and processes'. It is complemented by Article 18, Sub-section 2, which states that 'the Commission may at any time, in consultation with the State Party concerned, send special advisory missions to provide assistance to that State Party for strengthening its electoral institutions and processes'.

Within the Electoral Assistance Portfolio, the DEAU has undertaken a series of projects focused on EMBs, aimed at sharing best practices, creating regular exchanges and undertaking necessary reforms to improve the capacities of EMBs. The activities undertaken are regional training for EMBs, capacity building and forthcoming projects within a framework of horizontal cooperation in collaboration with the Organization of American States, aimed at peer exchanges of best practices between African and Latin American EMBs. Lastly, in order to remedy the absence of an AU framework for post-election observation, the DEAU will implement post-election audit workshops in any sub-region in which three elections have been held in the past six months. These workshops will enable a stocktake of an EMB's performance during the elections. These actions will allow the AU to follow up on the recommendations made by EOMs.

Despite the growing number of activities being implemented, the work of the AU in the field of technical and governance assistance has been somewhat limited compared to the work carried out on election observation. The main reason for this limited involvement is the scarcity of funding that the DEAU can dedicate to such assistance projects. In this sense, electoral assistance by the AU is still in its initial stages. However it is worth noting that the AU is gaining an increasing role in responding to the challenges entailed in building sustainable democracies on the continent.

In future years, the AU will extend its work on technical assistance from enhancing the institutional capacity of EMBs to developing the institutional capacity and democratic culture of political parties and designing electoral systems that broaden representation, recognize diversity, and respect equity and majority rule while at the same time protecting minority rights. These areas of activity are a priority because when political parties lack a clear commitment to democracy and their interparty relations are marked by intolerance and a disregard for electoral rules and codes of conduct, this can contribute to political tensions which can trigger election-related conflicts before, during or after elections. In addition, civil society organizations, including faith-based organizations, will be supported in their various efforts to strengthen democratic culture, in particular through voter education, civic education and conflict management initiatives (African Union 2010).

Conclusions

This chapter has presented developments and the accomplishments of the AU in the fields of democratization and, in particular, election observation and assistance. Since the 1990s, the OAU and then the AU have progressively increased their role and mandate with regard to protecting and promoting the integrity of elections. The AU currently operates under a clear and effective legal and institutional framework for electoral observation and assistance, further articulated since the entry into force of the African Charter on Democracy, Elections and Governance in February 2012.

Since the 1990s, the OAU/AU has observed close to 250 elections in a majority of its member states and has implemented important programmes for technical assistance and governance through the DEAU.

However, notwithstanding the marked progress that has been made by the AU and its member states in the field of democracy promotion and ensuring the integrity of elections, the recent upsurges of electoral violence in Côte d'Ivoire, Kenya and Zimbabwe testify to the need to further strengthen the democratic processes and structures of the AU member states. This will need to be done with tailored interventions in those member states which are still plagued by political violence and conflicts.

The AU will substantially contribute to this end by augmenting its interventions and programmes in the field of electoral technical assistance and governance support. In addition to its current programmes promoting effective and efficient election administration and management through capacity-building projects for EMBs, the AU will orient its technical support to a broader range of domestic actors, including political parties, and the design of electoral systems that broaden representation, recognize diversity, respect equity and ensure that majority rule respects minority rights.

The journey towards deepening and consolidating democratic governance in Africa is ongoing and open-ended. Now that the African Charter on Democracy, Elections and Governance has entered into force the AU must convince its member states to domesticate it. The Charter is to date the most comprehensive commitment by the AU member states to democracy, the integrity of electoral processes and good governance.

Finally, the AU, through the DEAU, is moving towards dedicating more resources to the implementation of its programmes on technical and governance assistance. Strengthening the institutional capacities of the EMBs, promoting a democratic culture among political parties and assisting with the design of electoral systems will contribute not only to the integrity of elections but also to the defusing of election-related conflicts and political tensions.

References

APRM Secretariat, *The African Peer Review Mechanism (APRM)* (Midrand, South Africa, 2003)

African Union (AU) Panel of the Wise, 'Election-related Disputes and Political Violence: Strengthening the Role of the African Union in Preventing, Managing and Resolving Conflict', The African Union Series, New York, International Peace Institute, July 2010

AU, 'Interim Report of the Chairperson of the Commission on the Prevention of Unconstitutional Changes of Government though Appropriate Measures and Strengthening the Capacity of the African Union to Manage Such Situations', AU, Sirte, July 2009

AU, Declaration on Democracy, Political, Economic and Corporate Governance of the New Partnership for Africa's Development (NEPAD), AU, Addis Ababa, 2002a

AU, *Guidelines for African Union Electoral Observation and Monitoring Missions*, AU, Addis Ababa, 2002b (mimeo)

AU, OAU/AU Declaration on the Principles Governing Democratic Elections in Africa, AU/OAU, Addis Ababa, 2002c (mimeo)

AU, Protocol to the African Charter on Human and Peoples' Rights on the Rights of Women in Africa, AU, Addis Ababa, 2003

AU, African Charter on Democracy, Elections and Governance, AU, Addis Ababa, 2007

Beaulieu, Emily, 'Interregional Organizations and Election Integrity: Resolving Conflict and Promoting Democracy', Background paper for the workshop 'Regional Organizations and Integrity of Elections', organized by International IDEA, Stockholm, 14–15 December 2011

Garber, Larry, 'The OAU and Elections', *Journal of Democracy*, 4/3 (July 1993), pp. 55–59

Hammerstad, A., 'African Commitments to Democracy in Theory and in Practice: A Review of Eight NEPAD Countries', AHSI Paper (June 2004)

Lopez-Pintor, R., 'Election Observation: Twenty Years of Learning', *Miradas al Exterior* (January 2010)

Lopez-Pintor, R., 'Reconciliation Elections: A Post-Cold War Experience', in Krishna Kumar (ed.), *Rebuilding Societies After Civil War: Critical Roles for International Assistance* (Boulder, CO.: Lynne Rienner Publishers, 1997)

Melber, Henning, AU, 'NEPAD and the APRM: Democratization Efforts Explored', *Current African Issues,* 32 (July 2006)

Mozaffar, S. and Schedler, A., 'The Comparative Study of Electoral Governance: Introduction', *International Political Science Review,* 23/1 (January 2002), pp. 5–27

Mwanasali, Musifiky, 'From Non-Interference to Non-Indifference: The Emerging Doctrine of Conflict Prevention in Africa', in J. Akokpari, A. Ndinga-Muvumba and T. Murithi (eds), *The African Union and its Institutions* (Auckland and Cape Town: Jacana Media and Centre for Conflict Resolution, 2008)

National Endowment for Democracy (NED), Final Report, 'OAU Elections Training Program' NED Core Grant 92-4 (2540)

Novicki, M., 'Interview with Salim Ahmed Salim,' *Africa Report* 36 (May–June 1992)

Organization of African Unity (OAU), African Charter on Human and Peoples' Rights, OAU, Addis Ababa, 1981

OAU, Declaration on the Political and Socio-Economic Situation in Africa and the Fundamental Changes Taking Place in the World, OAU, Addis Ababa, 1990a

OAU, African Charter for Popular Participation in Development, OAU, Addis Ababa, 1990b

OAU, Treaty Establishing the African Economic Community, OAU, Addis Ababa, 1991

OAU, Cairo Agenda for Action, Addis Ababa, 1995

OAU, Grand Bay (Mauritius) Declaration and Plan of Action on Human Rights in Africa, OAU, Addis Ababa, 1999

OAU, Lomé Declaration on the Framework for an OAU Response to Unconstitutional Changes of Government, OAU, Addis Ababa, 2000

OAU, 2000, Protocol to the Treaty Establishing the African Economic Community Relating to the Pan-African Parliament, OAU, Addis Ababa, 2000

OAU, Conference on Security, Stability, Development and Cooperation (CSSDCA) Solemn Declaration, OAU, Addis Ababa, 2000

Pretorius, J., *African Politics: Beyond the Third Wave of Democratization* (Cape Town: JUTA, 2008)

Strom, M., *Promoting the African Charter on Democracy, Elections and Governance: A Four-Part Guide for Study Circles* (Pretoria: IDASA, 2009)

Tazorora, T. G. Musarurwa, *Creating Sustainable Democracy in Africa: An African Supranational Body for the Effective Supervision of Elections in Africa* (Pretoria: University of Pretoria, 2008)

Notes

[1] The Organization of African Unity (OAU) was established in 1963. It evolved into the African Union after the adoption in July 2000 of the Constitutive Act of the African Union, which entered into force in 2001. The Constitutive Act of the African Union replaced the 1963 OAU Charter.

[2] Groups of people had previously monitored the outcome of specific elections on-site from the period of the Crimean War up to the 1980s in Uruguay, El Salvador and Chile (Lopez-Pintor 1997, 2010).

[3] In this respect, Secretary General Salim Salim asked the African American Institute (AI) and the National Democratic Institute (NDI) to develop training programmes for OAU staff from 1992. See National Endowment for Democracy (NED), Final Report, *OAU Elections Training Program*, NED Core Grant 92-4 (2540); and Garber (1993).

[4] 'Governance Challenges in Africa and the Role of the African Union', Public Lecture to mark the 20th Anniversary of the European Centre for Development Policy Management, 19 December 2006 (European Institute for Public Administration, Maastricht), by Amb. J. K. Shinkaiye, Chief of Staff, Bureau of the Chairperson African Union Commission.

[5] See Novicki (1992), p. 36. It is important to note that one of the first official documents calling for a greater involvement of the OAU in electoral observation and in democratization processes is the Report of the Secretary General on the

Process of Election Monitoring by the OAU issued during the 64th Session of the Council of Ministers, held in July 1996 in Yaoundé, Cameroon.

[6] In line with the principle of non-interference, the OAU had to be formally invited to observe elections by its member states. In addition, the mandate of each election observation mission was carefully negotiated between the OAU and the host government. The typical election observation mission included ambassadors from OAU countries and one or two OAU staff members. This team of observers reported to the OAU Secretary General. The election observation reports were shared with the government of the country involved, but not always with the wider public (Garber 1993).

[7] Although AU heads of state adopted the Charter in January 2007, it only entered into force after the February 2012 AU summit, 30 days after its ratification by 15 member states. Notably, of the 54 member states of the AU, only 39 had signed the Charter as of December 2011.

Chapter 2

Giving ASEAN a Role in Philippine Elections: The Case for Regional Participation in Deepening Democratization Processes

Chapter 2

Julio S. Amador III[1]

Giving ASEAN a Role in Philippine Elections: The Case for Regional Participation in Deepening Democratization Processes

Introduction

Southeast Asia is significant as a focus for international politics because of its potential for both conflict and cooperation. Analysing political phenomena at the regional level is important because 'The regional level is where the extremes of national and global security interplay, and where most of the actions occur' (Buzan and Wæver 2003: 43). Regional integration processes lead states to create regional organizations, the functions of which generally include providing an organized avenue for diplomatic dialogue and interstate cooperation. Regional organizations are important in many ways. One of the main purposes of regional organizations is what Edward Best and Thomas Christiansen (2008) call the management of interdependence, because these regional organizations seek to guarantee peace and security and reduce conflict, and to promote economic cooperation and social interaction among states. In Southeast Asia, the most enduring regional organization is the Association of Southeast Asian Nations (ASEAN), which was established in 1967.

ASEAN has evolved from an association whose basic goal was to preserve regional stability to one that has, in many respects, reflected the aspirations of the peoples living in its different member states. The ASEAN Charter, which was ratified by all member states in 2008, contains the various aspirations that motivate the development of ASEAN as a regional organization. Several of these aspirations include principles that involve democracy, good governance, the rule of law, human rights and fundamental freedoms (Article 1, purposes; and Article 2, principles), including the creation of an ASEAN Human Rights Body (Article 14). However, before 2012 ASEAN had not been actively involved in the election processes of its member states. The outcome of national elections within member states is sometimes reported and analysed in news reports because of the potential impact of the policies of the successful candidates on ASEAN. These reports are generally silent, however, on the role of ASEAN as a regional organization in national elections. The only time ASEAN has taken any action in relation to national elections is in response to the situation in Myanmar.

Elections are important because they provide avenues for political accountability, which is at the core of the democratization process. In practice, elections are a procedural aspect of democracy. Holding them does not in itself mean that the will of the people is being reflected or followed: democracy is deeper than elections. Nonetheless, how elections are conducted plays a major role in how the international community, national stakeholders and its citizens perceive a state. If states hold elections that are free and fair, investors and other states can believe that the government in power can be trusted. This goodwill may translate into increased trade or more aid.

It has long been conventional wisdom that regional organizations should not play a role in national elections because states have no business being involved in each other's political processes. Non-interference is a key norm in the practice of sovereignty. This chapter asks whether regional organizations should play a role in their member states, if only to foster opportunities for skills, knowledge and technology transfer. In particular, it:

1) examines the institutional context that might allow ASEAN to participate actively in deepening democracy within its member states by providing a clear analytical framework for the relevant context and mandate of ASEAN in the field of electoral observation and support in line with the ASEAN Political-Security Community (APSC) Blueprint;
2) provides an overview of the current practices of ASEAN in the field of elections, specifically electoral observation and support;
3) argues that ASEAN as a regional organization should be invited to act as an observer of the conduct of elections in the Philippines to help the country deepen its democratization processes; and
4) identifies comprehensive electoral support policies that could be pursued by ASEAN to promote and protect the integrity of elections.

The Philippines was chosen as a case study primarily because it is still deepening its democracy. It regularly conducts elections which are tainted with news of violence and allegations of cheating. However, it is also open to international observers. If the Philippines were to consent to invite in official observers from ASEAN, this would have two important impacts. First, it would make the Philippines more active in preventing disruptions and preserving the integrity of elections; and, second, it would provide avenues for other ASEAN member states to learn from its experience and perhaps adopt electoral processes that would move them towards greater openness and accountability to their own people.

A brief overview of elections in the Philippines

The Philippines has held free elections regularly since the fall of the Marcos dictatorship in 1986. These elections, however, have been characterized by reports of fraud and violence, especially in, but not limited to, rural areas in the far-flung islands of the archipelago. Nevertheless, the Philippines has several significant accomplishments in the field of electoral reforms. These achievements highlight the capacity of the Philippines to reform its electoral processes in response to citizens' demands and the changing social and political environment. One of the most significant accomplishments is its active partnership with civil society to promote free and fair elections.

The National Movement for Free Elections, which later became the National Citizens' Movement for Free Elections (NAMFREL), was founded in 1951 as a 'non-partisan election monitoring group, in time for the 1951 elections, to help deter and prevent election fraud' (Calimbahin 2010). In 1986, NAMFREL provided an alternative, more credible count of the votes because the official Commission on Elections (COMELEC) was seen as compromised by the government in power (Calimbahin 2010). According to Calimbahin, COMELEC suffered from a 'credibility deficit' during this period and the public looked to NAMFREL not only to protect the ballot but also to provide a credible count of the votes.

Another significant achievement by the Philippines in the conduct of elections is its pioneering of parallel vote tabulation (PVT) or quick count (Estok, Nevitte and Cowan 2002). NAMFREL is credited as the originator of the PVT process, whereby 'observers watch the voting and counting processes at specifically selected polling stations, record key information on standardized forms and report their findings (including the polling station's vote count) to a central data collection center' (Estok, Nevitte and Cowan 2002). PVT allows observers to validate the official tabulation of votes, which helps to expose divergences in vote counts as well as other irregularities. NAMFREL has been accredited as a non-governmental partner of COMELEC to conduct PVT, although in the 2010 elections the Parish Pastoral Council for Responsible Voting was selected instead. The PVT activities of non-governmental election 'watchdogs' have become accepted practice in the conduct of elections in the Philippines and are seen as a powerful tool for keeping elections free, fair and credible.

The Overseas Absentee Voting (OAV) Act was signed into law in 2003, enfranchising Filipino migrant workers based in other countries. Although OAV has been criticized in some quarters as a very expensive activity, it remains one of the most innovative election reforms in the region. For a developing country such as the Philippines, OAV is one way of ensuring that all its citizens are given the opportunity to participate in the conduct of democratic activities such as elections.

The automatic election system already had a long history in the Philippines before it was fully implemented for the 2010 elections. Kimura (2010) documents the history of electoral automation in the Philippines and traces its origins to COMELEC's vision and strategy for the period 1992 to 1998: 'Operation Modernization and Excellence', or MODEX.[2] In this strategy, COMELEC aimed to collaborate with all relevant stakeholders, including policymakers and civil society organizations, to produce a legal and policy framework for adapting and modernizing the political process. The automation of elections has been slow and beset with various challenges, but there has nonetheless been steady and incremental progress which could further improve the service provided by COMELEC.

The state accredits non-governmental organizations (NGOs) to observe elections in accordance with Article VII, Section 52 (k), of the Omnibus Election Code. NAMFREL, as is noted above, has been a partner of COMELEC in conducting PVT as a complement to official efforts. The Philippines does not close its doors to international election observers: it welcomes them in order to demonstrate that it intends to conduct open and fair elections. Various groups have sent missions to the country to observe the conduct of elections. These groups have produced critical reports which highlight the difficulties encountered. A review of these reports indicates that there is an interest from outside in observing, learning from and collaborating with the government in order to improve electoral processes. International election observers have been supported by funds from international foundations and other international NGOs.

One of the most comprehensive reports on the 2004 elections was written by the National Democratic Institute for International Affairs (NDI). Representatives from that organization came to the Philippines to serve as electoral observers. The NDI has sent various delegations in cooperation with other organizations to observe elections in the Philippines since 1986 (NDI 2004). In 2007, the People's International Observers' Mission sent a delegation with members from Australia, Belgium, Canada, Germany, South Korea, Japan, Myanmar, the Netherlands, Norway, Scotland, Switzerland and the United States (The People's International Observers' Mission 2007).

The Asian Network for Free Elections sent observers to the Autonomous Region of Muslim Mindanao during the 2007 elections. The region is notorious for election-related violence, but ANFREL reflected in its report that it was difficult to determine whether alleged violations of human rights committed before the elections were related to the elections. The group fielded 21 observers to various parts of Mindanao to observe the elections and published a report which analysed different situations before and after the conduct of the polls (ANFREL 2007). The group also published a more comprehensive report on the conduct of the 2010 elections, during which it fielded 47 observers in cooperation with local groups (ANFREL 2010). COMELEC accredited all these organizations, which allowed them access to various regions and provinces as well as COMELEC offices.

Elections are essential to democracy, and democratizing states need to continually improve their processes to ensure that the voice and will of the people are reflected in the outcome when they choose their leaders. While the focus should rightfully be on those states which are undergoing transition from military-authoritarian leadership, advocates of democracy should not forget that there are states such as the Philippines which are continuing the democratization process. More than 20 years after the fall of the Marcos dictatorship, the Philippines still faces many challenges related to economic and political development. Among these challenges is ensuring that elections are free and fair. Without clean elections, the Philippines will not be able to deepen its commitment to democracy.

There are compelling reasons why ASEAN member states should learn from one another in improving the conduct of each other's elections. Election systems in the Philippines benefit from external observation and comments because it is in the interests of a democratic state to improve its processes to ensure that the rights of its citizens are not violated but promoted and protected. This chapter suggests going one stage further. ASEAN observers could bring an additional dimension to complement the contributions of domestic observation organizations, one that is different in kind from that of international NGOs—or indeed any observation by representatives of Western states. The institutional context and the policies that guide ASEAN, as well as a brief review of ASEAN's role and its potential to act as an election observer, are discussed below.

The ASEAN institutional context and policies

The ASEAN Charter contains a list of principles that member states are willing to commit themselves to. Most of the principles, found in Article 2, Section 2, of the Charter, strengthen and stress the commitment to non-interference in the affairs of fellow member states. Three principles stand out, however, and give hope to those who see ASEAN as more than just the diplomatic playground of the governments of member states:

1) enhanced consultation on matters seriously affecting the common interest of ASEAN;
2) adherence to the rule of law, good governance, the principles of democracy and constitutional government; and
3) respect for fundamental freedoms, the promotion and protection of human rights, and the promotion of social justice.

Hidden in the diplomatic language of item (1) is the concern of member states that internal instability in one member state will have repercussions for the region as a whole. This is why, even though non-interference is the norm, in reality ASEAN member states use unofficial channels and various consultative mechanisms to push wayward states to conform with accepted regional behaviour. Sometimes, ASEAN is able to express its concerns about what is happening in member states in public. An example of this is the expression of 'revulsion' by the Chair of the ASEAN Standing Committee, supported by other member states, at the violent suppression of street protests in Myanmar in September of 2007 (Wah 2007).

Item (2), meanwhile, aims to ensure that member states remain committed to democracy, or at least move towards further democratization taking account of the limits imposed by the current constitutional and institutional set-up in some member states. Even with the non-interference norm in place, ASEAN still seeks some semblance of order among its member states by focusing on their capacity to adopt and accept democratic principles, which include free and fair elections. As an example, in the 2010 elections in Myanmar, ASEAN leaders called for the conduct of fair and democratic elections in that country and urged its leaders to uphold their commitment to do so (BBC News 2010).

Item (3) in the list recognizes that the people of Southeast Asia enjoy certain fundamental freedoms, and that ASEAN member states must protect and uphold these rights, including human rights and social justice. Morada (2008) notes that non-democratic ASEAN member states are often disinclined to give their people more political space and often disregard calls for greater freedom of expression and the protection of individual rights. Nonetheless, ASEAN is slowly moving in a more positive direction. The ASEAN Socio-Cultural Community (ASCC) Blueprint places great emphasis on social justice, reducing the development divide between member states, and the promotion and protection of the rights and welfare of women and children. It mandates promoting and enhancing the participation of women in all fields and at all levels, including in politics and decision-making, as well as the socio-economic empowerment of women, incorporating a gender perspective into national and regional policies and enhancing the participation of women in programmes and projects. In addition, the ASCC provides for the establishment of an ASEAN commission on the promotion and protection of the rights of women and children (ASCC C.1).

More concrete commitments can be found in the APSC Blueprint. Although originally envisaged as a security community within ASEAN, the APSC takes account of the fact that political developments in the region affect not only security but also the standing of ASEAN member states in the community of nations. The APSC is one of the pillars of the ASEAN Community and serves as the operational plan for the ASEAN Charter in increasing community building (ASEAN 2009).

Part A of the APSC Blueprint, the political aspect, 'A Rules-Based Community of Shared Values and Norms', focuses on promoting cooperation in political development with the aim of strengthening democracy, enhancing good governance and the rule of law, and promoting human rights, the rights of women (Action 1.5 vii) and fundamental freedoms. All this aims to create a rules-based community of shared values and norms (ASEAN 2009: 6). Particular agendas and actions within the APSC Blueprint focus on democratization and good governance (found in agenda item A.1) and encourage cooperation on political development. Specific actions include: (a) holding seminars/workshops to share experience of democratic institutions, gender mainstreaming and popular participation; (b) endeavouring to compile best practices for voluntary electoral observation; and (c) promoting good governance, which includes the conduct of analytical and technical studies to establish baselines, benchmarks and best practices in various aspects of governance in the region, as well as promoting the sharing of experiences and best practices through workshops and seminars on leadership concepts and principles with an emphasis on developing norms on good governance. In the implementation of the Blueprint, ASEAN will also strive to promote and support gender mainstreaming, tolerance, respect for diversity, equality and mutual understanding (APSC, part II, paragraph 7); and undertake studies to promote gender mainstreaming in peace building, peace processes and conflict resolution (B 2.2 vi).

ASEAN seeks to promote the principles on democracy found in agenda item A.1.8. The actions specific to this agenda are to: (a) promote understanding of the principles of democracy among ASEAN youth in schools at an appropriate stage of their education; (b) convene seminars, training programmes and other capacity-building activities for government officials, think tanks and relevant civil society organizations to exchange views, share experiences, and promote democracy and democratic institutions; and (c) conduct annual research on the experience of and lessons learned on democracy, aimed at enhancing adherence to the principles of democracy (ASEAN 2009: 9).

ASEAN's plans to deepen democracy in its member states are both pragmatic and holistic. They are pragmatic in that they take account of the different political structures and situations found in the region. Any plans for a 'one size fits all' democratization process are bound to fail. They are holistic because ASEAN does not force its member states to adopt democratic institutions immediately but allows the political space for reform within member states. Thus, there are action plans aimed at strengthening relations between civil society and government and learning programmes available for the people; and dialogue is actively promoted among various stakeholders.

Good governance should not be far from democracy in ASEAN's calculations. The APSC Blueprint in a sense promotes the idea that democratic principles cannot be strengthened without the establishment of accountability processes. The APSC Blueprint recognizes the important role played by civil society and the private sector in strengthening and upholding good governance. The participation of other sectors of society, regardless of gender, race, religion, language or social and cultural background, is central to the democratization process as envisaged by ASEAN, and serves as the cornerstone of good governance. While critics may hold that the Blueprint is essentially the handiwork of the member states, and that this is generally also true for the ASEAN Charter, it is noteworthy that ASEAN has put its various commitments on paper, and that robust participation by other stakeholders in the implementation process will reinforce and deepen the democratization process and build good governance in the region.

ASEAN and elections

In the area of elections, ASEAN has committed itself to compiling best practices for voluntary election observation. The strongest manifestation of this was the first-ever ASEAN electoral management body (EMB) Forum, which had as its theme 'Inspiring Credible ASEAN Electoral Management Bodies', held in Jakarta on 3–5 October 2011.

ASEAN's first brief involvement in election observation was during the 2010 Myanmar elections. ASEAN leaders urged the then ruling junta to promote free and fair elections and offered to send observers to the region. Myanmar declined this offer but instead allowed election observers from the Yangon embassies of the ASEAN member states. After the elections, however, civil society groups and activists denounced the ASEAN Chair's statement praising the elections as a fulfilment of Myanmar's democratization goals.

In 2012, Myanmar took a step forward, inviting both ASEAN and its member states to send a small number of observers shortly before polling day to the block of by-elections caused by the appointment of members of the legislature to Cabinet posts and other incompatible positions. Although this exercise was very limited, it marked a step forward not only for elections in Myanmar but also for ASEAN's institutional engagement with electoral observation. In the past, it has been argued that to give ASEAN a role, even a passive one, would be an intrusion in the internal affairs of member states (after all, the regional organization was not meant to act as a supranational body that can interpose itself in the affairs of its member states). However, in pursuance of its own political goals of improving good governance and deepening democracy, ASEAN can and must play a role in national elections.

As a regional organization of states that share common principles, ASEAN could learn lessons from civil society groups and other NGOs, which organize field teams to serve as observers during elections. Sending delegates in an official capacity to act as observers would serve to strengthen the drive to achieve democracy in the region. In the case of the Philippines, the government and COMELEC could invite ASEAN to send observers, and ASEAN could nominate observers to be accredited by COMELEC. The accredited observers could then be sent to various regions and report back to ASEAN. Their reports would have the potential to help the Philippines and other ASEAN member states determine whether any future support should be provided to further strengthen electoral processes in the Philippines.

A further reason for fielding ASEAN observers would be that it would allow other countries to learn from the experience of the Philippines when they hold their own elections. They may be able to learn about improving election participation, crafting guidelines for international observers, including the development of an accreditation process, and how to reform their respective electoral institutions and processes. ASEAN observers could come from the EMBs of member states or from the ASEAN Secretariat.

The main obstacle that this proposal would encounter is the charge of external interference in the affairs of a sovereign state. Member states that are less open to dialogue with civil society and other stakeholders in the ASEAN community-building process might see any attempt at an official ASEAN role in national elections as an indirect challenge to their sovereignty. This issue is not insurmountable. If the Philippines were open to an ASEAN role in observing its elections and gained advantages because of this, other ASEAN member states might follow suit. This raises the question of how to give ASEAN a role.

Laying institutional foundations

In a speech to the EMB Forum in Jakarta, the ASEAN Secretary-General, Dr Surin Pitsuwan, recognized the problems faced by member states in implementing credible elections, noting that elections are among the most difficult activities undertaken by a state in peacetime. He identified costs, logistics and changes in technology as among the major challenges for ASEAN member states (Pitsuwan 2011). Pitsuwan recognized that there must be an exchange of knowledge at the ASEAN level among officials in EMBs as a way to enhance technology and knowledge transfer between member states.

The participants, who came from various sectors such as EMBs, NGOs, and national, regional and international civil society organizations, affirmed the importance of democracy as a universal value that must be supported by processes such as free, fair and legitimate elections. They also affirmed the importance of domestic and international election observation as a support mechanism for protecting the integrity of the electoral process, and raised the issue of increasing participation by people from vulnerable sectors of society, such as people with disabilities.

Other issues raised during the Forum were the need for better enforcement or adoption of regulations covering political parties and campaign finance, the problem of election-related violence, and the challenges of adopting and adapting the technology to be used during elections. The participants agreed to increase support to EMBs and strengthen electoral and democratic processes by laying the foundations for what they called a Southeast Asian Electoral Community, to be established in 2013.[3]

ASEAN's Secretary-General highlighted the political and policy hurdles that must be overcome if the regional organization is to be given any role in national elections. Participants also spoke of the significant challenges for regional cooperation in the conduct of elections and the inherent difficulties linked to establishing democratic institutions and strengthening democratic processes. Democratic institutions are necessary so that effective rules of conduct and behaviour that govern state agents and citizens can be set in the right direction. These institutions include representative governance, the establishment of political party systems and elections. Democratic processes for the most part are needed to maintain and strengthen institutions. These processes include campaign finance, electoral observation, developing the capacity of election managers and training potential political leaders.

The Forum recognized that current practices, including a purely national vision of the conduct of elections, are not sufficient to address the need for democratization across the region. Cooperation between and among the private sector, civil society, international and regional organizations, academia and government is necessary in order to further deepen democracy and improve governance. It also recognized that strengthening electoral processes will be a key action in the implementation of ASEAN's desire for greater democracy and improved governance in the proposed regional community. ASEAN as a regional community therefore has a stake and a role in the elections conducted by its member states.

If ASEAN is going to be active in observing national elections, the right institutions must be crafted and established. This will need a gradualist approach that takes account of the disparate situation of member states. A number of steps will be needed:

- Introduce regional norms for voluntary election observation. These norms might include the endorsement of the Declaration of Principles for International Election Observation and the Code of Conduct for International Election Observers. Other norms that might be considered include the acceptance of election observation as a legitimate activity by both domestic organizations and the ASEAN regional community.
- Update the APSC Blueprint to include stronger language on promoting cooperation among EMBs so that member states can either promote it as part of their own agenda or find ways for like-minded member states to cooperate formally.
- Organize a sectoral body for EMBs to provide them with a regular forum for the exchange of ideas and best practices. Such a body could serve as election observers or as facilitators in selecting the election observers, who

could be accredited by ASEAN to the national EMB. The composition of election observers should, as far as possible, achieve gender parity.
- Request assistance from other international institutions such as International IDEA to facilitate the process of compiling best practices for voluntary electoral observation, as stipulated in the APSC Blueprint. Technical and financial assistance should be requested and welcomed by ASEAN.
- Encourage and support academic and policy research institutions to further study and develop practices for election observation within ASEAN. Track II dialogue will be important since various initiatives have already been undertaken to study democracy and democratization in ASEAN member states at this level. Including the study of and discussions on elections and electoral observations on the agenda of Track II will not be problematic in this regard. Further research on other issues related to elections, such as gender-related issues and mainstreaming, could be done at the Track II level when election studies have been integrated at this level of cooperation.
- Reserve some of the funds available in the ASEAN Secretariat to support studies, research and workshops on the development of voluntary electoral observation guidelines, reducing election-related violence and mainstreaming gender into the elections of member states.
- Encourage workshops that promote interaction between civil society, academia and EMBs to foster confidence building and promote goodwill, bearing in mind that future practical cooperation may rest on such personal contacts.

These proposals are not earth-shattering, but nor are they easy wins. In the context of ASEAN, policy proposals need to be carefully vetted in the national capitals before they can be discussed at the regional level. In the case of providing a role for ASEAN in the electoral processes of its member states, while its overall framework clearly gives ASEAN a role in democratization and good governance, the Blueprint on the Political-Security Community is highly conservative as it only provides for the compilation of best practices for voluntary elections observation.

The process must be started simultaneously at the regional and the national levels. At the regional level, there must be recognition that ASEAN's community-building efforts require greater emphasis on democracy and good governance. Both principles can only be strengthened when each member state establishes and maintains institutions that contribute to the overall political development of the people of Southeast Asia. Credible elections enhance the democratic aspirations of ASEAN, and a regional role is therefore not unwarranted but should be welcomed. At the national level, member states must be willing to accept observers and other technical assistance from each other. Member states should study and adopt comprehensive rules for election observation that comply with international standards.

In a regional community, excluding other states from contributing anything to each other's national and political development will not strengthen bonds of camaraderie but weaken the community ideal. ASEAN member states should recognize that accepting democracy and good governance as community principles carries with it demands for better and more credible institutions and a desire for greater participation in the political life of nations. Credible elections are at the centre of a credible democratization process. That is not to say that elections alone guarantee democracy, but credible elections help to strengthen that democracy.

Thus, for example, the Philippines should consider inviting in and hosting official observers who have been endorsed by ASEAN to observe their national elections. Embassies in Manila have already been active in providing election observers, and COMELEC has an established accreditation process which could be used for election officials and managers from ASEAN member states. Clear frameworks would be needed as well as explanations as to why ASEAN would be fielding election observers and what the added value would be for both the Philippines and the ASEAN member states.

Elections are important democratic institutions. However, holding elections is no guarantee that a state is democratic. There have been many instances of elections being corrupted to serve the interests of individuals and regimes, and to consolidate their hold on power. Nonetheless, the need for elections in the democratic process cannot be denied. Elections are the fundamental procedural aspects of a democratic polity through which the people demand accountability from their leaders. Election observation as an activity is therefore crucial to the overall protection and promotion of the right of the people to vote and stand in legitimate and credible elections.

Conclusions

The management of interdependence requires that states that seek to form a regional community commit themselves to the ideals and principles that will form the core of the future development of that community. As a regional organization is formed, structures and institutions must be crafted, nurtured and developed to respond to the needs of the people in its member states. In the case of ASEAN, its formation as a purely stabilizing organization and its transformation into a nascent community for the people of Southeast Asia tells a story of states and their people that are willing to search for new pathways to improve the lives and conditions of individuals living in the region.

Amid challenging political and economic circumstances, ASEAN has sought to forge a community based on common values. Among these are good governance and democracy. To ensure that the envisaged ASEAN Community is meaningful to its people, concrete mechanisms have been crafted to achieve these common aspirations. It is time for ASEAN to become more involved in the activities of its member states. Laying the foundations for cooperation in improving the credibility of electoral exercises in member states would be a substantive but achievable goal for ASEAN. The challenge is to overcome the distrust of neighbours and see that there are common interests in preserving the democratic aspirations of ASEAN. Political institutions such as elections should be promoted, developed and protected in order to guarantee their credibility and acceptability to people in Southeast Asia.

References and further reading

ANFREL, 'ANFREL Observation of the 2007 Philippine National Election in the Autonomous Region of Muslim Mindanao (ARMM)', *Asian Network for Free Elections*, 15–17 May 2007, available at <http://www.anfrel.org/report/philippine/philipine_2007/PH_MINDANAO.pdf> (accessed 11 October 2011)

— 'The Philippines: Automated National and Local Elections', *Asian Network for Free Elections*, 10 May 2010, available at <http://anfrel.org/country/The_Philippines/Mission_Reports/2010/PH_2010_Final.pd> (accessed 11 October 2011)

ASEAN, *Roadmap for an ASEAN Community 2009–2015: One Vision, One Identity, One Community* (Jakarta: ASEAN Secretariat, 2009)

ASEAN Secretariat, 'ASEAN Chair Issues Statement on Myanmar Elections', *ASEAN*, 11 November 2010, available at <http://www.asean.org/25580.htm> (accessed 6 October 2011)

BBC News, 'ASEAN Leaders Issue Burma Election Call', BBC, 9 April 2010, available at <http://news.bbc.co.uk/2/hi/asia-pacific/8611930.stm>

Best, Edward and Christiansen, Thomas, 'Regionalism in International Affairs', in John Baylis, Steve Smith and Patricia Owens (eds), *Globalization of World Politics: An Introduction to International Relations* (Oxford: Oxford University Press, 2008)

'Burma Bars Foreign Reporters and Monitors from National Election', NTD Television, 19 October 2010, available at <http://english.ntdtv.com/ntdtv_en/ns_asia/2010-10-19/811451706324.html> (accessed 6 October 2011)

Buzan, Barry and Wæver, Ole, *Regions and Powers: The Structure of International Security* (Cambridge: Cambridge University Press, 2003)

Calimbahin, Cleo, 'Capacity and Compromise: COMELEC, NAMFREL and Election Fraud', in Yuko Kasuya and Nathan Gilbert Quimpo (eds), *The Politics of Change in the Philippines* (Pasig: Anvil Publishing, 2010)

Estok, Melissa, Nevitte, Neil and Cowan, Glenn, *The Quick Count and Election Observation* (Washington, DC: National Democratic Institute for International Affairs (NDI), 2002)

Kimura, Masataka, 'ICT and Reform in Electoral Administration: An Assessment of Philippine Electoral Modernization', in Yuko Kasuya and Nathan Gilbert Quimpo (eds), *The Politics of Change in the Philippines* (Pasig: Anvil Publishing, 2010)

Morada, Noel M., 'ASEAN at 40: Prospects for Community Building in Southeast Asia', *Asia-Pacific Review*, 15/1 (2008), pp. 36–55

National Democratic Institute for International Affairs (NDI), 'Report on the 2004 Philippine Elections', August 2004, available at <http://www.ndi.org/files/1745_ph_elections_083104_body.pdf> (accessed 10 October 2011)

Pitsuwan, Surin, Message by Dr Surin Pitsuwan, Secretary-General of ASEAN, at the ASEAN Electoral Management Bodies' Forum, 'Inspiring Credible ASEAN Electoral Management Bodies', ASEAN Secretariat, October 2011, available at <http://www.asean.org/26648.htm> (accessed 10 October 2011)

The People's International Observers' Mission (IOM), 'Final Press Statement', Center for People Empowerment in Governance, 18 May 2007, available at <http://eu-cenpeg.com/piom/april2010/IOM%202007%20Press%20Statement%20May%2018%202007.pdf> (accessed 10 October 2011)

Wah, Chin Kin, 'Introduction: ASEAN – Facing the Fifth Decade', *Contemporary Southeast Asia*, 29/3 (2007), pp. 395-405

Notes

[1] The author is indebted to Atty Dashell Yancha-Po, Raul Cordenillo and Eleonora Mura for their comments and insights on this chapter. All the opinions contained in this chapter are those of the author and do not reflect the official stance of the Philippines Foreign Service Institute.

[2] For a comprehensive discussion of the history of election automation in the Philippines see Kimura (2010).

[3] For more details, see the Jakarta Declaration on Southeast Asian Electoral Community 2011, which is the outcome document of the First ASEAN EMB Forum held in Jakarta, Indonesia, 3–5 October 2011.

Chapter 3

The Evolution of Election Observation in the European Union: From Fraud Prevention to Democracy Support

Chapter 3

Domenico Tuccinardi, Franck Balme
and Gillian McCormack

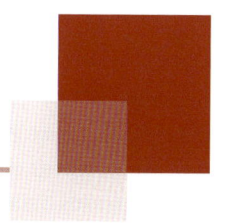

The Evolution of Election Observation in the European Union: From Fraud Prevention to Democracy Support

Introduction

International election observation has come a long way during more than 20 years of continuous activity. From the unstructured activities that took place in the 1960s and 1980s, which often served to rubber-stamp elections, through the hard lessons learned in the early 1990s, international election observation evolved in the new millennium to become a serious and rigorous undertaking, and is now widely recognized as a crucial instrument for democracy support. Enthusiastic support for the second and third democratization waves in Eastern Europe and many countries of Sub-Saharan Africa, Latin America and Asia led to a number of large-scale international election observation missions (EOMs) focused on election day. These were sometimes blurred with the electoral assistance activities of wider United Nations (UN) peacekeeping missions. Others were organized on a bilateral basis by former European colonial powers invited in by the autocratic regimes ruling their former colonies. One of the principal motivations for European Union (EU) involvement in election observation was the need for its member states to avoid falling into the trap presented by bilateral mechanisms that were, often with good reason, perceived as biased by the new political forces. However, beyond this, the EU system offered a strong basis for an impartial assessment of the crucial multiparty elections that were mushrooming at the beginning of the 1990s. Article 6 of the Treaty on Economic Union, now Article 1 of the Lisbon Treaty, placed the protection and promotion of human rights and democracy at the heart of the EU mandate and central to all its development cooperation policies.

The EU deployed its first observation mission to Russia's first multiparty elections in 1993, by an ad hoc decision under the Common Foreign and Security Policy (CFSP) pillar. Other ad hoc CFSP decisions followed to observe the first post-apartheid elections in South Africa in 1994 and the first democratic elections in the West Bank and Gaza in 1996. More ad hoc decisions, sometimes under the CFSP, sometimes by the European Commission, provided the basis for electoral observation and assistance in Bosnia, Albania, Mozambique, Nicaragua, Togo, Nigeria and Indonesia.[1] In almost all cases, these efforts, despite attempts to examine the larger legal framework around elections, were limited in scope and focused almost exclusively on elections as a single event. This was in line with the major declared outputs of observation activities at the time, which were to ensure that the will of the voters on election day was respected and to increase confidence in the elections. The limited scope of these EU observation efforts was also related to the way in which the EU's involvement in many of these processes was designed, with electoral observation included as a political complement to wider support to the logistical and technical organization of the electoral processes.

Following the experiences of those early years, and thanks to the efforts of the Office for Democratic Institutions and Human Rights of the Organization for Security and Co-operation in Europe (OSCE ODIHR), as well as non-governmental organizations (NGOs) such as the National Democratic Institute (NDI) and the Carter Center, EU EOMs developed into a more professional, rigorous and long-term undertaking, characterized by serious analysis of the nature and quality of the implementation of the legal framework underpinning the elections and of the political environment surrounding them. In 2000, those experiences were finally codified in an official Communication (European Commission 2000), which sets out the rationale and methodology for EU election observation and assistance interventions—the document is still in force today. A crucial change in the professionalization of activities was the introduction of an annual planning mechanism and centralized programming and implementation services, which replaced the ad hoc decisions and structures of the 1990s. In elaborating the EU observation methodology, the EU drew largely on the lessons learned by the OSCE ODIHR in its own area of intervention. In the Communication, election observation is defined as a political complement to electoral assistance, managed separately to guarantee independence of judgement. Election observation is described as 'the purposeful gathering of information regarding an electoral process, and the making of informed judgments on the conduct of such a process on the basis of the information collected, by persons who are not inherently authorized to intervene in the process' (International IDEA 1997: 10). In both political and technical terms, this approach marked a clear watershed from the experiences of the 1990s. Since 2000, the EU and all the major international EOMs, although no longer necessarily characterized by the participation of hundreds of short-term observers, have witnessed an enormous growth in scope, duration and sponsoring organizations, making important contributions to peaceful and democratic development.

As a consequence of these successes, international election observation became a fashionable and visible instrument often used to promote Western efforts in support of democratic movements. It was also sometimes overrated as a mechanism for deterring fraud and other irregularities, or promoting public confidence in the electoral process and mitigating conflicts. In recent years, international election observation has witnessed a further evolution, becoming a sophisticated and complex mechanism of democracy support. The nature of this evolution is demonstrated by the scope and quality of assessments and reports, and the average duration of EOMs in the new millennium. This evolution is mainly a consequence of a better understanding that democratic processes 'do not unfold in a set sequence of stages' (Carothers 2002) and that electoral processes are composed of 'a number of integrated building blocks, with different stakeholders interacting and influencing each other' (ACE 2008: 15). The aim of this chapter is to highlight some of the key developments in internal election observation since 2000, and its emergence as a democracy support instrument in EU external policy, and to discuss how and whether this instrument can remain an effective part of the EU strategy for democracy promotion in the post-Lisbon Treaty setting.

The Declaration of Principles for International Election Observation

The global evolution of international election observation is well encapsulated in the Declaration of Principles for International Election Observation.[2] After two years of preparatory work led by the NDI and the Carter Center in cooperation with United Nations officials, and with the active involvement of a number of other organizations, this document was officially endorsed in 2005 by representatives of 22 organizations at a ceremony hosted by the United Nations on 27 October 2005, and led by then UN Secretary-General Kofi Annan. It remains open to future endorsement. For the EU, participation in the drafting of the Declaration of Principles served as an important means for taking stock of and crystallizing a number of changes introduced by Communication 191/2000, as well as reflecting on those aspects of its observation work that fell short of the endorsed principles, promoting a process of continual reflection.

The Declaration of Principles now guides the practice of all major international EOMs. It can serve as the basis for negotiating memoranda of understanding between international EOMs and the election commissions of countries inviting them, and it is used in several countries to determine the regulations and procedures that should govern relations between election administrators and election observers. It has enhanced communication, cooperation and collaboration among key electoral management bodies (EMBs) and their national and international partners in a large number of countries, rationalizing and streamlining the contribution to democratic development. Since its adoption, the Declaration has been signed by 39 organizations, which meet annually to reflect on the degree to which their observation activities have been faithful to its principles. The process that surrounds these annual meetings has become as important as, if not more important than, the principles enshrined in the Declaration itself. It is a form of self-regulation which raises awareness and promotes coordination among election observation organizations all year round, one in which they confront their challenges and shortcomings. This now semi-permanent process is mainly characterized by a striving for accountability. Participants share their thinking on how to overcome the difficulties of observing under pressure from sometimes corrupt political parties and institutions and of placing the need to put their impartiality ahead of the risks of promoting instability and perhaps even fuelling conflicts. The continuous reflection on the challenges surrounding election observation promoted by the annual implementation meetings has greatly assisted an overall demystification of the work of international election observation, acknowledging its many limitations but also its unique prerogatives and highlighting the need for it to complement other democracy assistance tools in order to be truly effective.

Many of the organizations that have endorsed the Declaration of Principles have subsequently made significant efforts to upgrade their observation methodology and evaluate its value in their overall democracy promotion strategies—encouraging their peer organizations to do the same. An important example in this respect comes from the Organization of American States (OAS), which has in recent years produced a number of important studies on the long-term aspects of election observation (media monitoring, gender analysis and political party finance analysis), changing its overall conceptualization of election observation and assistance—both of which now form part of the work of its Department of Electoral Cooperation. In addition, the OSCE ODIHR regularly organizes methodological workshops and frequently expands its EOMs to include experts in gender and human rights and, where necessary, new voting technologies. The EU is currently updating its guidelines on the analysis of women's participation in electoral processes with a view to mainstreaming gender analysis into every EU mission's overview and recommendations.

No longer just 'free and fair'

One of the most emblematic results of this critical reflection on the impact of international election observation has been the demise of the catchphrase 'free and fair' from the language of EOMs. This apparently simple change in the language and style of observation reports represents a major achievement in clarifying for public opinion the extent of what international observers can and cannot do. The Inter-Parliamentary Union's Declaration on Criteria for Free and Fair Elections, and the related seminal study which codified for the first time in international public law the criteria and conditions for democratic elections (Goodwin-Gill 1994), gave this phrase a life of its own and immense media prominence in relation to election observation. For over 15 years, many national and international stakeholders believed that the role of international election observation was to attest to the issue of whether elections were free and fair, and felt let down when observers' answers were more nuanced and complex.

Political scientists and election specialists have for many years tried to come up with an agreed formula for what constitutes 'free and fair' that all can agree on, but without success. As early as 1997, Elklit and Svensson noted that: 'The phrase "free and fair" cannot denote compliance with a fixed, universal standard of electoral competition; no such standard exists, and the complexity of the electoral process makes the notion of any simple formula unrealistic' (Elklit and Svensson 1997). Eric Bjornlund (2004) dedicated an entire book to a deconstruction of this belief: 'Measuring elections against a free and fair standard suggests a dichotomy—that elections either pass or fail a test of legitimacy—when elections are actually political processes more realistically judged along a continuum and placed in context'. Notwithstanding these significant early contributions to the understanding of election observation, the phrase 'free and fair' remained an irresistible temptation for many EOMs seeking to grab easy headlines—at least until the adoption of the Declaration of Principles. The fact that this set of principles exists is a reminder that election observation is a more complex undertaking, entailing the 'systematic, comprehensive and accurate gathering of information concerning the laws, processes and institutions related to the conduct of elections and other factors concerning the overall electoral environment; the impartial and professional analysis of such information; and the drawing of conclusions about the character of electoral processes based on the highest standards for accuracy of information and impartiality of analysis'.[3]

For EU EOMs, abandoning this expression signified acknowledgement of two notions: first, that there is no perfect election and each process has shortcomings to be addressed; and, second, that it is not the task of election observation to validate an electoral process, but rather to offer a genuine and impartial assessment of what was observed in a spirit of cooperation with the partner country, with a view to fixing the flaws for future elections. This process corresponded with an understanding that the evaluation of an electoral process is a complex undertaking that cannot be encapsulated in a simplistic 'thumbs up or thumbs down' manner. A 2008 briefing paper for the European Parliament put it this way: 'After 15 years of international election observation, with increased awareness of election standards and observation methodology, subjective and simplistic "free and fair" statements have lost credibility. The particular problem with the "free and fair" formula is that it only allows a black/white evaluation, while the quality of an election is mostly in a grey zone between fully in line with international standards and fundamentally flawed' (European Parliament 2008: 13).

This process has taken place in parallel with a policy shift in EU-sponsored electoral assistance programmes away from event-driven to process-driven types of support, with a growing awareness of the need to integrate electoral observation and electoral assistance activities into a wider cycle of democracy support initiatives. Despite all this, the question of free and fair elections remains very appealing to the media. The question opens the door for international observers to explain their methodology to the public in an accessible way, placing their analysis in the wider and long-term context of democracy support.

What international standards?

A second ongoing demystification process that has helped place international election observation in a proper context, and is related to the annual discussions on the implementation of the Declaration of Principles, is the progressive abandonment of another catchphrase. This one became the most frequently used expression in election observation reports: 'international standards for elections'; but what are these international standards for elections? Is this just a semantic problem that can easily be overcome when it is made clear that observation missions assess electoral processes against the provisions of international and regional treaties?

The Declaration of Principles makes scant use of the phrase, encouraging a more complex reflection on the central value of election observation assessments. Moreover, the annual meetings on the Declaration of Principles, and the research work that informs them, have highlighted the ambiguities and disadvantages of referring to international standards for elections as benchmarks for the work of international observers.

The term 'international standard' is a measurement applied to the acceptability, quality and accuracy of an electoral process by international organizations that are often perceived in the host countries as Western-oriented. Such standards are neither universal nor binding. In many of the countries in which observers operate, references to such standards trigger an automatic rejection of the observers' assessments, because these standards do not take account of the national and regional context. In reality, the problem is even greater as the use of the phrase is not only confusing but 'blurs the binding nature of international obligations and commitment for elections . . . the phrase "international standard for elections" weakens election observation because it disguises the binding nature of election-related obligations that countries have voluntarily accepted' (Meyer-Ohlendorf 2010).

There are in fact no agreed standards for regulating or implementing electoral processes around the world, as there is no specific form of democracy that can be considered superior to any other. The fundamental freedoms to be upheld are defined in the 1948 Universal Declaration of Human Rights, the 1966 International Covenant on Civil and Political Rights and many other international and regional treaties. The practical ways in which such freedoms are protected can take several forms, according to the context as well as cultural and social traditions. The acceptance of this tenet is key to an appreciation of the potential value of electoral assistance and observation, as well as the benefits of their synergized actions for democracy development—especially for a global development actor such as the EU.

In this context, it is the research and development work undertaken by the Carter Center, as a way of taking the Declaration of Principles forward, that has shed the most significant light on the place of fundamental obligations on democratic elections in public international law.[4] The initiative aims to establish common criteria for assessing elections and recognizes that election observation should be understood in the context of, and closely linked to, broader efforts to promote democracy, with elections as unique opportunities to assess how well a country's political institutions serve its citizens. In a thorough review of sources of public international law, the Carter Center research identified 21 meta-obligations on democratic elections and assessed the degree to which each of these obligations has a direct impact on observers' understanding of a particular part of the electoral process. This new approach to election observation is being embraced by a growing number of organizations and has become the basis for designing new types of observation techniques, which seek to analyse the gap between host country national legislation, its implementation on the ground and the overarching international obligations subscribed to by the host country. This approach also demonstrates the synergies between election observation and election assistance, and how both can only make sense if offered in a spirit of partnership and cooperation in an attempt to support the host country, which has invited the observation and agreed to be scrutinized in order to meet its international obligations.

The impact on EU election observation

The developments described above represent a critical change in the conceptualization of election observation and demand a continuing upgrade of its assessment methods, and also provide the only way for international observation to remain relevant as a democracy support instrument. Anchoring election observation assessments to existing obligations that are legally binding on host countries, and subscribed to by those countries through their signature and ratification of international and regional treaties, leaves the countries concerned with no room for discretion regarding adherence. It is not about imposing standards, but about helping countries to meet their own international obligations while at the same time acknowledging that there are several different ways to achieve this. This tenet must be more clearly expressed when describing the mandate of international observers, so that host countries have a clear expectation of the type of contribution that will be made by international observation.

A ground-breaking policy shift is currently taking place that is making election observation a central instrument of democracy support. This is particularly true for the EU election observation system. The European Council Conclusions of November 2009 explicitly mention election observation as one of the key '…dialogue instruments that can address elements related to democracy support',[5] as well as the need to use those instruments in a more coherent and integrated way. This evolution determines that the focus of election observation is no longer exclusively on fraud prevention, denunciation of electoral malpractice, confidence building and conflict mitigation. The final reports are at the centre of the new EU strategy for election observation, designed to be forward-looking assessments of the state of democracy and human rights in a partner country that has requested this service, and based on the specific international obligations to which each host country has subscribed.

In this context, it is important to build on the conception of electoral observation and electoral assistance as separate but complementary instruments serving the same democracy support purposes, both provided in a spirit of partnership and respect for the national ownership of the host country. This concept was introduced in Communication 191/2000, but only fully developed into a coherent policy in the November 2009 Council Conclusions and more recently in the De Keyser Report (European Parliament 2011). In the UN context, although these two activities have not been conducted simultaneously for almost a decade, increased attention is being paid to the recommendations of observer groups as an important component of UN cyclical technical assistance to electoral processes, and there is full acknowledgement in key documents of the synergies between electoral assistance and electoral observation.[6] More generally, there is an increased trend towards post-election coordination among international actors as well as increased involvement of development cooperation agencies in this dynamic.

Those institutions that deploy or sponsor EOMs while also providing technical electoral assistance (mainly the EU, the NDI and the Carter Center) are becoming much better at harmonizing the programming of electoral assistance and observation activities in an independent but synergetic manner. This means that election observation recommendations have the potential to become fundamental documents that influence the type of support that international actors interested in promoting democracy can negotiate with partner countries within the respective frameworks of their cooperation treaties. While such synergetic action does not yet take place systematically, there has been progress in the past five years and the way is now paved for much more effective and concerted action. In this context, the most important contribution of international EOMs lies in the provisions of their final reports and the recommendations they contain. In recent years, the Final Report has been transformed from a bureaucratic and formal step to end the mission to a potential instigator of a new political dialogue and cooperation cycle. It represents a snapshot of the state of democracy in the host country, and documentation of the gaps that exist between international obligations and the domestic legal framework, and between the domestic legal framework and implementation practice observed on the ground. From this perspective, the recommendations become the real legacy of EU EOMs. In analysing the impact of this modern form of election observation, it is therefore paramount to take account of the development cooperation principles for aid effectiveness (ownership, alignment, harmonization, results and accountability),[7] which institutions sponsoring or deploying EOMs have undertaken to comply with, as well as the commitments enshrined in the Declaration of Principles. It will then be important to determine how distant implementation and the outcomes of EOMs are in practice from all these statements, using the same methodology that EOMs use in their assessment of electoral processes against international commitments on democratic elections.

The formulation of concrete recommendations that are useful for the purposes described above is a tall order for EU election observation, but nonetheless a primary goal. Inserting international observers' recommendations into domestic reform processes implies primarily an acceptance of the need to coordinate and negotiate these with a number of national actors: national legislators, domestic civil society, political parties and assistance providers on the ground. This type of work requires the development of a methodology and a discipline that differ from those currently applied by international observation groups during the assessment process, as well as the more sophisticated and multi-pronged political strategy requested in the De Keyser Report (European Parliament 2011). Another ingredient that will be indispensable in order to achieve these aims is much closer cooperation with regional and domestic observation groups.

The underrated value of domestic election observation

The significance of the work of domestic observation groups is, from a global perspective, still rather underrated by electoral support providers. Domestic election observation activities are at the heart of the development of a flourishing election observation sector. Domestic observation methods have been evolving for 25 years. They involve highly complex and scientific tools that cannot be utilized by international observers, such as parallel vote tabulation (PVT), voter registration audits and political party finance monitoring.[8] Experiences such as those of the National Citizens' Movement for Free Elections (NAMFREL) in the Philippines in 1986 and Transparencia Perú in 2000 have been instrumental in and exemplary for the creation and subsequent development of international election observation. Many other significant developments in domestic observation have taken place in, for example, Chile, Croatia, Indonesia, Montenegro, Serbia, Sudan, Zambia and Zimbabwe. This experience, however, while giving international prominence and media attention to election observation, has not been used to achieve the coherent growth of domestic observation groups in other parts of the world.

One of the collateral, but potentially most important, effects of the Declaration of Principles has been to put the focus back on the work of domestic observation groups. This resurgence in interest has also motivated domestic observation groups to come together in a global network to reaffirm in a more formal and assertive manner their own overall commitment to impartial observation, to promote democratic reforms in their respective countries and to take advantage of the benefits of systematic peer collaboration. This has recently produced a new, unifying set of commitments: the Declaration of Global Principles for Nonpartisan Election Observation and Monitoring by Citizen Organizations.[9] This document was discussed and drafted under the auspices of the NDI and benefited from its dual experience as a key drafter of the Declaration of Principles and as a major provider of technical assistance to domestic observation groups around the world. Regional networks of domestic observers also played a fundamental role in systematizing practices and sharing valuable experience.

Many domestic observer groups have suffered—often unfairly—from a poor reputation and consequently have not attracted the type of support that had been envisaged at the beginning of the new millennium. A number of factors led over time to a generalized mistrust of domestic observer groups: a lack of funding, the poor quality of their reports, poor-quality public outreach strategies, a perceived or genuine political bias, and bad methodologies. A perceived lack of professionalism inspired suspicion on the part of governments, EMBs and political parties, which saw these groups as troublemakers, revolutionaries or counterproductive activists. The prominence of international EOMs, which highlighted election day, also overshadowed the work of domestic observer activities, which took place during the pre- and post-electoral periods, and made them less attractive to international funders. It was often difficult for domestic observers to become an effective force for dialogue or promoters of democratic reform. However, as election days became increasingly 'cleaner' or less rigged, the need to observe other critical phases of the electoral cycle became more important. Components such as voter registration, boundary delimitation, complaints and appeals, political party finance, electoral campaign expenditure and results tabulation required greater attention as they became growing sources of disputes.

Despite the recent emphasis on longer-term observation, international EOMs will always be rather limited in this area. Only domestic observer organizations are truly capable of conducting long-term observation throughout the electoral cycle and reporting directly on the pre- and post-electoral phases. The increasing importance of the role of domestic observers as necessary actors in safeguarding the electoral process as a whole should lead to greater technical and financial support by international donors. Funding has allowed domestic observer groups to develop new, more rigorous observation methodologies and improve their capacity to carry out efficient EOMs. There are indications that in future the duration and capacity of international observation missions may appear so limited, in comparison to the work of domestic groups, that they will play an increasingly minor role. For the EU, a more consistent approach to supporting domestic observation activities will certainly be needed if it is to fulfil its declared intention to implement a fully holistic approach to democracy support. This is particularly the case given the insurmountable structural limitations of its own observation activities in key electoral areas, such as voter registration, political party finance and vote tabulation. A decisive strengthening of the support provided to domestic observation activities is coherent with one of the declared long-term strategic objectives of EU election observation which is often mentioned but never fully acted on—to build impartial national observation capacity that makes its own observation activities redundant (European Commission 2000: 16).

Domestic observers and observation around the electoral process

The Declaration of Global Principles for Nonpartisan Election Observation and Monitoring by Citizen Organizations provides an important set of values for self-awareness and accountability among non-partisan election monitoring organizations, in a very similar fashion to the process established for international observation. More importantly, it provides a basis for understanding which non-partisan organizations can engage with electoral stakeholders and international actors, paving the way for more effective forms of cooperation between international and domestic observers. Domestic observers have gained a clearly defined place in the electoral process over the years by playing an active role with all stakeholders.[10] Impartial domestic observation brings many potential benefits to an election process.

Domestic observers make the electoral process more accessible to the general population by keeping *voters* informed—conducting civic education campaigns, using the Internet and social networks—and by underlining the strengths and weaknesses of the different phases. This generates a cascade effect: greater transparency strengthens public confidence in the process and encourages the population to participate in the different steps of the election. Domestic observers can give a voice to citizens and make each voter a potential observer. During the 2008 elections in Kenya, domestic observers inspired the creation of the *Ushahidi* (witness in Swahili) software and website to map reported incidents of post-electoral violence. Information was submitted by citizens using the website or their mobile phones. This technique, known as 'crowd-sourcing', has been used by domestic observers in several recent elections, including in the Philippines, Sudan, Uganda, Liberia and Mexico, to record incidents of violence or fraud and offer immediate feedback to national institutions and electoral authorities.

Domestic observers can play an active role in mediating where there is a confrontational political context, by calling for a peaceful campaign or inviting *political parties* to sign a code of conduct. By monitoring party finances, electoral campaign resources and expenditure, domestic observers effectively deter corruption by political parties and candidates through the threat of exposure. They can ensure that all political parties have equal or equitable access to public resources for campaigning or to convey their messages in the media. Domestic observers can help build the skills of political parties in conducting their own observation of the process; for example, they can train them to conduct their own PVT by sharing their methodology.

Fruitful collaboration between domestic observers and *EMBs* increases the level of transparency in the electoral process and strengthens public confidence in it. Domestic observers can also alert EMBs to problems or potential problems before the elections. They can assist EMBs by providing ongoing feedback on the implementation of election procedures nationwide. Domestic observer groups conducting long-term observation can issue interim reports and discuss them with election officials prior to election day so that problems can be remedied. This essential element represents a significant departure from the mandate of international observers. In a cooperative working environment, a PVT conducted by domestic observers can back up the EMB's elections results, especially in a context where the counting and tabulation take some time. The role of domestic observers can be crucial for EMBs in highly polarized societies in which there is a need for an independent voice to generate consensus among political players on the rules of the electoral game—particularly on the acceptance of results.

The growing role of domestic observers cannot be ignored by international EOMs. The need to observe the entire electoral cycle requires a close collaboration in which both parties can benefit from each other's analysis in different fields. The potential advantages of cooperation are manifold. For international observers, domestic observer groups can provide a much-needed longer-term perspective on events that have taken place long before the international mission arrived. Domestic observers are best placed to lobby for and monitor the implementation of the electoral reforms initiated, following a collaborative process, by departing international missions. Cooperation with international groups may well strengthen confidence in the professionalism and impartiality of domestic observers in the eyes of electoral stakeholders.

New types of collaboration can also be envisaged in the future: joint international and domestic EOMs. In the observation of the 2010 elections in Afghanistan, the NDI included local observers in its international observation team, which had a positive effect on the quality of the overall analysis. The growing opportunities that are offered for representatives of domestic observer groups to participate in international observation missions in other countries are strengthening their technical expertise and enlarging the horizons of domestic observation experts, as they see their experience as a valuable asset outside their own countries and of specific importance to regional organizations engaged in observation.

The regional dimension of international observation

Organizations such as the NDI and the Carter Center paved the way for new forms of cooperation in election observation. In the meantime, other organizations have become active in involving representatives of domestic observation groups in their international observation missions: the Electoral Institute for Sustainable Democracy in Africa (EISA), Acuerdo de Lima, the European Network of Electoral Monitoring Organizations (ENEMO) and the Asian Network for Free Elections (ANFREL). Two common features among these groups are their distinct regional focus and their increasing credibility in their respective regions.

The specific nature and credibility of regional organizations, which are at the intersection between international actors and their national counterparts, gives them the potential to provide the most interesting and innovative avenues for integrated democracy building. Among the most important functions that they already carry out is their mediation and monitoring role after peace agreements and political deadlocks. This mediation and monitoring mandate could be taken advantage of more often during election observation activities, especially for the implementation of observers' recommendations and improving coordination. The impact of observers' recommendations in post-electoral political dialogue is still rather limited and remains a major challenge for international observation. One of the most frequently mentioned causes of the limited impact of the recommendations of EU EOMs is their perceived lack of contextual understanding. Regional organizations are uniquely placed to promote continuous dialogue on the implementation of recommendations and to facilitate the understanding of national interlocutors of the necessary reforms to meet regional and international obligations. The experiences of horizontal cooperation in Latin America facilitated by the OAS and the Centro de Asesoría y Promoción Electoral (CAPEL, Center for Electoral Promotion and Assistance) provide a significant example of the potential role of regional organizations in this area, and illustrate how they could become the ideal conduit for the EU to make its own international observation activities redundant in the long term.

In terms of election observation coordination, the need for increased cooperation between international and domestic observers often faces a number of practical implementation issues. International missions are often deployed late. They need to become operational very quickly and interaction with domestic observers is not a priority. A simple courtesy visit or meeting might be the entire collaboration. In addition, sometimes the will to preserve the integrity of the mission limits the ability of international observers to take into account the domestic observers' findings. Time constraints often prevent better interaction with domestic observation, but prejudice is still a factor in many cases. The Declaration of Global Principles for Nonpartisan Election Observation and Monitoring by Citizen Organizations will help to reduce doubts and residual prejudice. However, a lack of knowledge about domestic observers' activities, a lack of trust and misperceptions sometimes lead international observation missions to ignore local organizations. Supporting the efforts of regional organizations involved in election observation might help reduce this type of problem from both ends, while still offering sponsoring organizations the required guarantees of neutral assessments, as well as appropriate and expeditious contextualization and understanding of domestic circumstances.

The EU has reaffirmed the need to strengthen cooperation with regional organizations as an objective in improving the effectiveness of its human rights and democracy support external action (European Union 2011).[11] Cooperation on election observation activities, capacity-development programmes and experimentation in joint EOMs represent immediate and easily achievable ways to give such declarations of intent a concrete implementation perspective.

In addition, there are opportunities for cross-fertilization and regional peer-learning that only regional structures can provide. In this context, national experiences and apparent contradictions and deviations from internationally accepted practices can be filtered and analysed through lenses that have a specific understanding of regional issues as well as the supranational credibility that is often needed to bring observation assessments to the attention of national stakeholders. Last but not least, regional organizations are in a perfect position to promote respect for the commitments spelled out in regional treaties.

Conclusions

International election observation has evolved significantly since the 1990s. It has become a complex undertaking and a meticulous assessment of the legal framework for elections in the host country at a highly specific moment in time, the electoral period, while also encompassing various components of the larger democracy realm within the assessment.

Thanks to the process that surrounded the endorsement of the Declaration of Principles and the continued efforts of several institutions that organize EOMs, election observation is no longer exclusively focused on highlighting the democratic standards that a specific electoral process has fallen short of. Instead, it concentrates on assessing the degree to which the obligations related to democratic elections to which a given partner country has subscribed are being met, both in legislation and in the more practical administration of the electoral process. This is done taking a positive and forward-looking approach, with a desire to contribute to the democratic evolution of the partner country.

Provided that a number of steps are taken in the future programming and implementation of its EOMs, EU election observation efforts have the potential to evolve and mature further in order to play a more meaningful role in the democratic development of partner countries. *The EU should:*

1) **Complete the change to more holistic and process-oriented assessment missions.** The EU must engage in the observation process only when the conditions for a long-term presence in a host country are guaranteed. This type of long-term engagement should not necessarily be linked solely to the pre-electoral period, but must guarantee the length of time and resources needed to produce a thorough assessment of the process in the light of international and regional obligations.

2) **Emphasize the role of international and regional obligations as a central guide to observation assessments.** The significant progress made in recent years in showing that international obligations on democratic elections are clearly extrapolated from international treaties and other sources of public international law needs to continue and be consistently implemented in all observation activities, including in the activities of long- and short-term observers. Understanding the importance of local context and that a variety of good implementation

practices exist does not diminish the need to anchor the mission's assessment in objective and internationally binding principles.

3) **Build the observation around its most important output: the recommendations.** EU observation missions must be focused around their main declared aim, and include in their ranks the necessary technical and political expertise to be able to produce concrete, relevant and achievable recommendations, share their findings and approaches with regional and domestic observers, and be prepared to adjust their recommendations (but not their findings) after this dialogue to ensure that they are locally owned and compatible with the cultural and social tradition of the partner countries.

4) **Embark more decisively on fuller cooperation and mixed missions with regional and domestic organizations.** If the institutions sponsoring and deploying international election observation are serious in wanting to bolster the concept of observing the process and not the event, there is no alternative but to enhance international–domestic observation cooperation. The role of many domestic observation groups across the globe as promoters of democracy and active citizenship rights beyond the election period should be the model to aspire to and support, rather than those cases where domestic observation is still hijacked by the political interests of specific factions. The end goal is to make domestic observation sustainable and reduce international observation to post-conflict situations where not enough trust can yet be placed in national actors.

5) **Achieve better integration of parliamentary representatives within international EOMs.** The possible negatives presented by 'rogue parliamentarians' are outweighed by the advantages of a parliamentary presence in election observation, in terms of both media attention and political understanding of the larger democracy picture of which elections are just a part. The more often parliamentarians are included in international observation missions, the higher their level of understanding and respect for 'international observation mission rules of engagement'. Particularly in the post-electoral period, when there is often a window of opportunity with newly elected legislatures, parliamentarians could have a greater role to play with their newly elected peers in ensuring a more impactful follow-up process. This makes particular sense in the EU system, given its unique potential for following up its own observers' recommendations in the political dialogue with its partner countries.

6) **Invest significantly in follow-up activities, balancing technical and political interventions in the partner countries.** Since the endorsement of the Declaration of Principles, much has been

accomplished in terms of dialogue on follow-up, and several endorsing organizations have made this a central priority of their work. In practice, however, the implementation of observers' recommendations has lagged behind. There is a clear need to enhance follow-up visits to present and discuss findings with partner countries' institutions and civil society as well as more post-election mid-term assessments to assess and help partner states meet their international and regional commitments. There are many voices in favour of having smaller observation missions but a continued presence in the partner countries throughout the electoral cycle in order to adjust observation practice to the widely recognized concept of being process-driven.

7) **Enhance inter-institutional cooperation in the follow-up process.** No organization sponsoring or deploying international EOMs can lay claim to a continued high level of resources in every country in which it engages. There is therefore a need to establish mechanisms to guarantee a continued presence and political dialogue. The follow-up process needs to start immediately in the post-election period in order to seize any potential opportunity for dialogue with the new legislature, even though it might yield fruit only years later. These windows of opportunity are often a passing train that requires a continuous presence and monitoring in order to catch it. As international development actors cannot sustain a constant high level of engagement or presence, it might be more appropriate to involve regional organizations in this specific dialogue process.

References

ACE, 'Focus on Effective Electoral Assistance', International IDEA, Stockholm, 2008

Bjornlund, Eric, *Beyond Free and Fair: Monitoring Elections and Building Democracy* (Washington, DC: Woodrow Wilson Center Press, 2004)

Carothers, T., 'The End of the Transition Paradigm', *Journal of Democracy*, 13/1 (2002)

Elklit, Jorgen and Svensson, Palle, 'What Makes Elections Free and Fair?', *Journal of Democracy*, 8/3 (July 1997)

European Commission, Commission Communication 191/2000

European Parliament, 'Election Observation: Achievements and Challenges', Foreign Affairs and Development Committee, June 2008

European Parliament, 'Report on EU External Policies in favour of Democratisation', Report 2011/2032 (INI) (also known as the De Keyser Report)

European Union, Joint Communication 886/2011, 12 December 2011

Goodwin-Gill, Guy, *Free and Fair Elections: The Development of International Law and Practice* (Geneva: Inter-Parliamentary Union, 1994)

International IDEA, 'Code of Conduct for the Ethical and Professional Observation of Elections', International IDEA, Stockholm, 1997

Meyer-Ohlendorf, Nils, 'Forget International Standards', DRI Discussion Paper no. 2, November 2010, available at <http://www.democracy-reporting.org/files/internationalstandards_discussionpaper_2.pdf>

Notes

[1] More information on the history of EU involvement in election observation can be found in Annex 1 of Commission Communication 191/2000.

[2] The Declaration of Principles for International Election Observation is available on a number of the websites of the sponsoring and endorsing organizations, including the NDI and the Carter Center.

[3] Principle 4 of the Declaration of Principles on International Election Observation.

[4] The Carter Center research and the related database are available at <http://www.cartercenter.org/peace/democracy/des.html>.

[5] The European Council Conclusions on Democracy Support in the EU's External Action are available at <http://www.consilium.europa.eu/uedocs/cms_Data/docs/pressdata/en/gena/111250.pdf>.

[6] See the United Nations Secretary-General's biannual reports on enhancing the effectiveness of the principle of periodic and genuine elections and the promotion of democratization; and General Assembly Resolution 62/150.

[7] These principles were endorsed in the Paris Declaration of the Second High-Level Forum on Joint Progress toward Enhanced Aid Effectiveness (Harmonisation, Alignment, and Results), available at <http://www.oecd.org/document/43/0,3746,en_2649_3236398_34430443_1_1_1_1,00.html>.

[8] For a full review of domestic observation methodology tools see the NDI website, available at <http://www.ndi.org/elections?page=0%2C1#NonpartisanDomesticMonitoring>.

[9] This document was officially endorsed on 3 April 2012 by representatives of 150 domestic observation groups and is available at <http://www.gndem.org/declaration-of-global-principles>.

[10] A comprehensive review of the areas of engagement by domestic observation groups is available on the website of the Global Network of Domestic Election Monitors at <http://www.gndem.org/resources>.

[11] See European Union, Joint Communication 886/2011 of 12 December 2011.

Chapter 4

The League of Arab States and the Electoral Gap

Chapter 4

Amor Boubakri

The League of Arab States and the Electoral Gap

Introduction

The League of Arab States (Arab League) is a regional intergovernmental organization that was created just a few months after the Second World War. Its creation was the result of rising Arab nationalism, which at the beginning of the 20th century had brought Arab leaders together to fight against the Ottoman Empire with the aim of achieving the political unification of the Arab countries in a Pan-Arab state (Salem 1962: 289–99; Seabury 1949: 633– 42). The original project of a Pan-Arab state was never realized, however, and instead a pan-Arab organization was created with a mandate to strengthen cooperation between the independent Arab states. Respect for each member's sovereignty was one of the fundamental principles on which the Arab League was built (Barnett 1995).

The founding member states of the Arab League were Egypt, Iraq, Jordan, Lebanon, Saudi Arabia, Syria and Yemen. These were the only independent Arab states at the time the League was created. The Arab League currently has 22 member states.[1] The people of these countries are bound by a common culture based on Islam and Arabism. However, it should be noted that some of the Arab League member states are not Arab countries, and that other religions and cultures exist in the region.

The struggle for independence and the construction of the post-colonial Arab states led in the majority of cases to the installation of autocratic regimes, which often lasted for many decades. A number of Arab states have only recently started to hold regular, recurrent and competitive elections. Previously, citizens did not have the opportunity to participate in the public life of their countries or to choose their own representatives. Elections were often limited to the local level, while membership of the national parliament was often based on the 'co-optation rule', by which parliamentarians were summarily appointed by the executive branch of the government. In the Sultanate of Oman, for example, universal suffrage was introduced for the first time only in October 2003 to elect the Majless Al-Shura (a representative council) (Herb 2004).

Even in the Arab countries in which elections have taken place for decades, people have rarely had an opportunity to express their will freely. Elections have often been uncompetitive and lacked both transparency and fairness. These elections perpetuated one-party rule (Posusney 2002). A 2002 joint report by the United Nations Development Programme and the Arab Fund for Economic and Social Development on human development in the Arab region demonstrated how the lack of political participation through transparent, competitive and recurrent elections has hindered the Arab people's capacity to achieve development and overcome social and economic problems (UNDP and AFESD 2002: 108–109).

In some cases, however, elections were respectful of the standards recognized by the international community. Moreover, the Arab revolutions (or Arab Spring as it is often called) resulting from the uprising in Tunisia in January 2011 are likely to produce significant democratic reforms and to foster competitive and recurrent elections in conformity with international standards. Democratic, free and fair elections have become a central demand of Arab citizens, who will no longer tolerate marginalization, oppression and autocracy.

The role of regional organizations in elections has been remarkable in recent decades. Some organizations, such as the Organization of American States (OAS) or the European Union (EU), have played a decisive role in different electoral processes not only in their respective regions but, in the case of the EU, also worldwide (Goodwin-Gill 2006: 36–51). Electoral assistance and observation are widely recognized as central instruments of democracy support. International organizations have often provided technical assistance to countries undergoing transitions from autocracy to democratic rule. Of particular interest in this field have been the assistance projects focusing on professionalizing electoral management bodies (EMBs). As in other regions, international organizations observing elections or providing technical assistance have become a common feature in the Arab region (Carapico 2008).

In this context, it is worth recalling the efforts of the Arab League with regard to electoral processes in the Arab region. In addition, it is interesting to examine the likely future role of the League in election observation and assistance after the Arab revolutions which have deposed autocratic regimes in order to build democratic rule. This chapter, before discussing the prospective role of the Arab League in election observation and assistance, explains the relationship between elections and democratization in the Arab region—a topic of worldwide concern in the decade since the events of 11 September 2001.

The Arab League and democratization in the Arab region

Democratization is a process that leads to a strengthening of civil liberties and an enhancement of political participation through free and fair elections. The process of evolving from autocracy to democracy involves several actors and requires a set of strategies and policies in order to peacefully consolidate progress (Whitehead 2002).

The Arab region did not experience what Huntington described as the third wave of democratization at the beginning of the 1990s (Huntington 1991). This process occurred at the end of the Cold War but did not affect the Arab region. Arab regimes did not undergo democratic reform at that time. Authoritarianism reached critical levels in the Arab region, and this was reflected in the lack of space for political participation and in violations of human rights. Observers and scholars have often remarked on the exceptionalism of the Arab world in the field of democracy, while criticizing the authoritarian regimes in the region and advocating the implementation of political reform.

Authors have developed several theories to explain the Arab World's democratic deficit, and these can mainly be summarized in two approaches. The first uses cultural and religious reasons to explain the chronic democratic deficit, while the second considers that this deficit is rooted in sociological and historical reasons.[2] As in other regions, authoritarianism in the Arab region has social, economic and political bases. Power is retained by a small elite which also controls the state's resources, and citizens are deprived of basic human rights and of the right to participate in public life. Elections often lack transparency and fairness.

Despite the only modest progress made by the Arab countries towards political reform, democratization processes have gained considerable importance on the agendas of Arab leaders in the past decade. This is related to the international context and to the role of the United States (USA), the EU and the United Nations (UN), which are committed to supporting the Arab countries to carry out genuine political reform (Brumberg 2002). The strong involvement by international actors can be explained as a reaction to the terrorist attacks on the USA of 11 September 2001.[3] Political reforms are considered key to making the change that the Arab world needs and to tackling the root causes of terrorism. For this reason, competitive elections became a priority of democratization programmes in the region (Carothers and Ottaway 2005; Sadiki 2009; Schedler 2002).

Reforms in the Arab world must address the weaknesses of the political systems, mainly by promoting an independent judiciary; effective political parties; competitive, internationally observed elections; and legislatures that represent majorities and can play a genuine role in scrutinizing the executive branch (Brumberg 2002: 57).

Traditionally, the Arab League has not contributed to fostering democratic reforms in the region, mainly because it has always lacked a clear mandate in the field of democracy and good governance. The first attempt to introduce political reforms on to the League's agenda was the elaboration of the 2004 Tunis Declaration. The discussions at the 2004 Arab League Summit in Tunis demonstrated the difficulty of putting such issues on the Arab League's agenda. Saudi Arabia and Mubarak's Egypt in particular were strongly opposed to any attempt to introduce reform programmes into the Arab League's work. Nonetheless, at the Tunis Summit, Arab leaders adopted the first multilateral Arab call for reform. Notwithstanding this great achievement, the Tunis Declaration was drafted in general terms and did not provide for concrete measures to be implemented. The language of the declaration mirrored the disagreements and the 'red lines' of its negotiators. According to the Declaration the Arab countries expressed their intention to:

> "[P]ursue reform and modernization…and to keep pace with the rapid world changes, by consolidating the democratic practice, by enlarging participation in political and public life, by fostering the role of all components of the civil society, including NGOs, in conceiving of the guidelines of the society of tomorrow, by widening women's participation in the political, economic, social, cultural and educational fields and reinforcing their rights and status in society, and by pursuing the promotion of the family and the protection of Arab youth (para. 2.3)."

The Tunis Declaration was reinforced by other regional documents such as the Doha Declaration for Democracy and Reform and the Alexandria Charter. The first was issued on 4 June 2004 at the end of a two-day conference hosted by Qatar University's Gulf Studies Center and supported by the Qatari government. It stresses constitutional reforms that could transform absolute monarchies into constitutional monarchies and circumscribe presidential powers in republics. The declaration also calls for free and fair elections. The Alexandria Charter was drafted by a group of 150 Arab intellectuals and issued on 14 March 2004 at a quasi-governmental conference supported by the Mubarak regime in Egypt. The Charter highlights the need for the transfer of power in Arab regimes to be through free, democratic and transparent elections. Notwithstanding the importance of these groundbreaking documents, they are non-binding. It is important to note, however, that these initiatives reflect a new state of mind in the region, where citizens and governments are both, but differently, concerned by the issue of reform. The course of events has recently opened the way to unexpected changes in the Arab region thanks to what is widely known as the Arab Spring. The Arab uprisings have demonstrated the will of citizens for reform and democratic rule, as well as the limits of autocratic rule. This general context explains the limits of the Arab League's role in the field of elections and the prospects for this role in the light of the current dramatic changes that are occurring in the region.

The Arab League and elections

A modest involvement

The Arab League's involvement in elections began with the deployment of an election observation mission (EOM) during the 1995 presidential elections in Algeria. Following this initial involvement, the Arab League observed the Algerian presidential elections in 1999, 2004 and 2009. During the same period, the League deployed observation missions in Comoros, Djibouti, Iraq, Lebanon, Mauritania, Sudan and Tunisia. Election observation missions have been carried out regularly since 1995. This new dynamism reflects the will of the Arab League to be involved in the process of political reform in the Arab region. The deployment of EOMs is a tangible confirmation of the Arab League's commitment to democratization and reform. Notwithstanding these important developments, however, it should be noted that the undertakings of the Arab League in the field of electoral observation and assistance thus far remain modest.

As is described above, the modest reach of the Arab League's action in the field of electoral observation and assistance is due both to the lack of a specific mandate in this field and to the fact that the member states of the Arab League have historically perceived election observation and assistance as exclusively state domains. The Arab League deploys EOMs only at the invitation of the member state holding the elections. It cannot monitor elections unless a member state explicitly requests the League to deploy an EOM (Meital 2006).

The legal and institutional framework

The legal framework

As is noted above, the Arab League currently lacks a clear legal and institutional framework in the field of electoral assistance and observation. The founding document of the Arab League, the Pact of the League of Arab States, signed on 22 March 1945, contains neither provisions on nor references to electoral observation and assistance. In this regard, it must be noted that the Pact does not attribute particular functions that would allow the League to assume political responsibility as a regional intergovernmental organization. The Pact mandates the League 'to draw closer the relations between member States and co-ordinate their political activities with the aim of realizing a close collaboration between them, to safeguard their independence and sovereignty, and to consider in a general way the affairs and interests of the Arab countries' (Article 2). This cooperation concerns in particular the economy and finance, communication, culture, health and social welfare.

For historical reasons related to the colonial pasts of the founding member states, the Arab League strictly adheres to the principle of non-interference in the internal affairs of its member states. In this regard, Article 8 of the Pact states that: 'Every member State of the League shall respect the form of government obtaining in the other States of the League, and shall recognize the form of government obtaining as one of the rights of those States, and shall pledge itself not to take any action tending to change that form'.

The adoption in 1994 of the Arab Charter on Human Rights was a milestone in the evolution of the Arab League (Al-Midani and Cabanettes 2006). The Charter provided that 'the people are the source of authority and every citizen of full legal age shall have the right of political participation, which he shall exercise in accordance with the law' (Article 19). However, the 1994 Charter never entered into force. In January 2001, the Arab Commission on Human

Rights recommended that the 1994 Charter should be revised, and in March 2003 the League of Arab States Council gave the Commission this task.[4] The work of the Commission culminated in 2004 when a revised version of the Charter was presented as part of an effort to 'modernize' the Arab League (Rishmawi 2010).

The 2004 Charter on Human Rights entered into force on 15 March 2008. The Charter established a specialist committee, the Arab Human Rights Committee, to supervise its implementation. In addition, a Sub-Committee on Human Rights was created in 2007 to assist the Arab League with preparing studies and drafting treaties. The Sub-Committee is made up of independent experts and is currently drafting an Arab Convention on the Rights of the Child.

Notwithstanding the importance of the Arab League's initiatives in the field of human rights, the Arab Charter on Human Rights does not address election observation and assistance. The undertakings of the Arab League in this field are therefore carried out on an ad hoc basis. As is noted above, the basis for the involvement of the Arab League in the modernization processes of its member states resides in the 2004 Tunis Declaration. It still lacks a comprehensive legal and institutional framework, however.

The Arab League's modest involvement in election observation and assistance diverges from the undertakings of other regional organizations in this field. Regional organizations such as the African Union (AU), the EU, the OAS and the Pacific Islands Forum (PIF) have progressively moved away from strict enforcement of the principle of non-interference in internal affairs to play a fundamental role in promoting and protecting the integrity of national electoral processes, subject to their respective mandates and membership. The AU has set up a comprehensive legal and institutional framework linked to its 2007 Charter on Democracy, Elections and Governance, which entered into force on 15 February 2012. The OAS adopted the 2001 Inter-American Democratic Charter. The EU's member states adopted the 2000 Charter of Fundamental Rights of the European Union. The PIF adopted the Biketawa Declaration in 2000. In addition to the above regional legal and institutional frameworks, the actions of the AU, the EU, the OAS and the PIF in international election observation have been guided by the 2005 Declaration of Principles for International Election Observation and by the Code of Conduct for International Observers, commemorated by different international organizations on 27 October 2005 at the United Nations in New York.

The institutional framework

As is noted above, the Arab League deals with election observation using ad hoc teams. Overall responsibility for coordination of the EOMs resides with the Political Affairs section of the League's General Secretariat. Within the Political Affairs section, the Arab Affairs Department has a dedicated unit in charge of election observation. Although this unit is in charge of deploying EOMs to all the Arab League's member states, in practice, when a mission is to be deployed to Arab-African countries (e.g. Comoros, Djibouti, Somalia and Sudan), the Arab-African Cooperation Unit is in charge of their coordination and deployment. This practice is motivated by the need to deploy French-speaking observers to Arab-African countries. In addition, in order to have coherent cooperation with the African Union, EOMs in Sudan and Somalia are also handled by the African Department. Thus, the two units have shared responsibilities with regard to election observation and the Arab League de facto distinguishes between EOMs deployed in Arab-African member states and EOMs deployed in Arab non-African countries. The League's Election Observation Head of Mission is usually a senior election expert from the Arab League. However, on several occasions, due to the political sensitivity of particular EOMs, the League's missions have been headed by political officials. This differentiation in the leadership of missions is often reflected in the observers' final reports. Missions led by political officials tend to produce more 'cautious' reports, while missions led by senior experts in elections have faced fewer constraints in assessing elections and thus made more effective recommendations on how to improve the electoral process in the countries monitored.[5] Neither of the departments involved in the coordination and deployment of EOMs has a mandate for electoral assistance.

There is a need for the Arab League to go beyond election observation and to start to implement programmes and projects under the broader category of electoral assistance, tackling the entire electoral cycle. There is also a need for a dedicated unit that can overcome the current ad hoc and operational division between Arab-African and Arab non-African countries within the Arab League's departments responsible for coordinating and implementing its undertakings on election observation and assistance.

Electoral assistance

Although it is true that neither of the units dealing with election observation has a mandate for electoral assistance, the Arab League has undertaken activities in the field of electoral assistance on two occasions. The Arab League worked in Comoros and, to a lesser extent, during the 2009 Mauritanian presidential elections. While the involvement of the League has been very limited, these two experiences are significant and reflect important developments that could frame Arab League policy in the future.

The Arab League provided the government of Comoros with continuous electoral assistance from 2006 to 2010. During the 2006 presidential elections, the Arab League helped to train polling station staff. In 2008 it assisted the authorities with the organization of two presidential elections. Furthermore, the role of the Arab League was not limited to election day, but extended to the post-election period.

In particular, the Arab League supported Comoros to overcome the crisis which occurred in the island of Anjouan. The mission of the Arab League continued its work until this conflict was resolved by the organization in 2009. The Arab League contributed to the budget of the Comoros Independent Electoral Commission, and the League's mission played an active role in supporting the Commission to organize the presidential elections.

The mission not only assisted the newly established Electoral Commission but also played an important role in the resolution of the conflict in Anjouan. Furthermore, the Arab League played an important role in co-organizing the subsequent constitutional referendum. It helped the political parties hold the constitutional forums that gathered the views of different stakeholders in order to deepen debate on the issues of governance and institutional reform in Comoros. The mission remained on the ground to help Comoros actors to overcome the emergency and deal with the post-referendum period.

The involvement of the Arab League in Mauritania encompassed electoral observation and was a form of longer-term electoral assistance to oversee the restoration of the constitutional order. The Arab League was a member of the committee monitoring the compliance of the Mauritanian authorities with the Dakar agreements. The Dakar agreements ended the crisis which occurred after Mohamed Abdelaziz's military putsch, which toppled the elected President, Sidi Ould Cheikh Abdallahi, on 6 August 2008.

The observation missions

As we have seen, election observation missions represent the core of the Arab League's action in the field of elections in the Arab region. These missions have been carried out on ad hoc bases without applying a standardized methodology and for this reason they have been often criticized as lacking effectiveness.

The geographical focus of election observation missions

The EOMs carried out by the Arab League have been limited to elections held in Arab countries. The League, like most other regional organizations, has until now refrained from observing elections in non-member countries, with only one exception—an observation mission sent to Ethiopia in 1990.

As of 2011, the Arab League had deployed EOMs to Algeria (1995, 1999, 2004 and 2009), Comoros (2002, 2004, 2006, 2007, 2008, 2009 and 2010), Djibouti (1999, 2003, 2005, 2008 and 2011), Iraq (2009 and 2010), Lebanon (2009), Mauritania (2007 and 2009), Sudan (2010) and Tunisia (2009).

The Arab League has not observed elections in Egypt, Jordan, Morocco or the Palestinian Occupied Territories, where electoral processes are often considered to be more competitive compared to the rest of the Arab countries (Posusney 2002). The Arab League did not deploy an EOM to the elections held in Tunisia on 23 October 2011, a few months after the revolution. From this brief account it is possible to conclude that Arab League EOMs have not been deployed homogeneously across the Arab region.

A focus on presidential elections

Most of the EOMs carried out by the Arab League focus on presidential elections. This is due to the presidential nature of the executives in the majority of its member states. Presidential elections are therefore the most important and sensitive elections in the great majority of the Arab countries. Observation missions were carried out exclusively to observe the presidential elections held in Algeria in 1995, 1999, 2004 and 2009, and in Mauritania in 2007 and 2009. EOMs were also sent to observe presidential and local elections in Comoros (2002, 2004, 2006, 2007, 2008, 2009 and 2010), as well as presidential elections in Djibouti (1999, 2005 and 2011), Sudan (2010) and Tunisia (2009, simultaneously with legislative elections).

A trend towards collaborative action

An emerging and increasingly common feature of the Arab League's EOMs is their cooperation with other organizations interested in observing elections in the Arab region. This collaborative culture began during the presidential elections in Djibouti in 1999. A joint observation mission was set up between the Arab League, the Organization of African Unity (OAU) and the Organization Internationale de la Francophonie (IOF). The joint mission was proposed by the IOF. Since 1999, the Arab League has carried out joint missions with other intergovernmental organizations to observe elections in Comoros, Djibouti and Mauritania. The Arab League has enlarged its network of partners to include the African Union, the Organization of the Islamic Conference, the Intergovernmental Authority on Development and the Arab Maghreb Union. This cooperation with different actors allows for the optimal use of resources. In addition, joint missions are important venues for exchanging expertise and sharing knowledge among peers, allowing the actors involved to learn from each other's best practices.

In order to deploy a joint observation mission, the parties involved have to sign an agreement. It has been common practice for the Arab League to identify potential partners and present a proposal to the organization identified. Cooperation with the African Union has become established practice in cases where the League has to observe elections in Arab-African countries. In this regard, the excellent coordination between the AU and the League in observing Algerian presidential elections is worth noting. After the joint mission agreement has been signed, the partners proceed to agree on the geographical areas that each team will cover, and which polling stations will be observed by each of the participating organizations.

The findings of the mission are announced in a public statement that usually covers both the positive and the negative aspects of the elections. To date, the participating organizations have not issued a common final mission report, but each organization has compiled an independent report.

Not all the international organizations approached by the Arab League have agreed to conduct a joint mission. The EU, for example, did not agree to observe the 2010 Sudanese presidential elections jointly with the Arab League. This can essentially be explained by the fact that the two organizations do not share the same methodology for conducting EOMs.

In addition to collaboration with intergovernmental organizations, the Arab League conducted EOMs in cooperation with the governments of China and France in 2010 to observe the presidential elections in Comoros. The Arab League also cooperated with the Libyan government to observe the Comoros referendum in 2009 and the 2010 governor elections in Anjouan.[6]

The main difficulties of the Arab League's observation missions

A lack of means

The high financial cost of deploying EOMs is one of the main challenges that regional organizations commonly face and the Arab League, like other regional organizations, suffers from a lack of adequate financial resources. In some instances, the League has agreed that observation missions can be funded by the host country. This was the case, in particular, for the EOMs sent to observe the Algerian presidential elections in 1995, 1999, 2004 and 2009. However, this practice undermines the independence and credibility of the Arab League's EOMs. Some of the League's staff declined to join observation missions funded by the Algerian government.[7]

Financial constraints have led the League to conduct short-term election observation missions that do not allow observers to witness the procedures for voter registration, or to monitor the media or the political parties' finances and campaigns. Arab League EOMs are deployed only a few days before election day and their stay does not cover the announcement of even provisional results.

The lack of adequate resources also affects the number of observers deployed. The EOMs are usually composed of ten experts. Given the geographical challenges posed by most of its member states, there is a need to increase the number of observers deployed. The Arab League often recruits external experts to support its own staff during an EOM. In such cases, it needs to guarantee that the additional observers deployed are equipped to carry out the required tasks.

A lack of guidelines

The absence of a standardized methodology or guidelines for conducting EOMs is a major challenge for the Arab League. Missions are run on an ad hoc basis. The lack of a standardized methodology is at the heart of several of the weaknesses that have had a negative impact on the Arab League's EOMs. In particular, EOMs do not produce detailed final reports in which fundamental aspects of the electoral process are assessed. Topics such as gender, ethnic participation, media monitoring and political financing do not form part of the analysis in the Arab League's EOM reports.

What role for the Arab League in future elections?

The Arab region is likely to undergo widespread electoral reform in the coming years. It is possible that the Arab countries will turn to international and regional actors for assistance and support in their reform processes. On the one hand, most Arab countries have to reform their electoral systems in order to be in line with international standards on democratic, free and transparent elections. As the demand for wider participation and enjoyment of political and civil rights increases across the region, governments must react and proceed with genuine reforms of their electoral systems. On the other hand, the Arab region is currently undergoing a crucial moment of political transformation. Despite the violence that has in some cases characterized this quest for change, the evolution of the transition in Tunisia, for example, confirms that Arab revolutions are paving the way for democracy.

Political reform has been the first step taken in the countries affected by revolutionary movements and also in neighbouring countries, where governments responded to the quest for reform in civil society in an attempt to avoid a fully-fledged revolution. Electoral reforms are likely to become a major concern for the Arab regimes in the near future. The Arab League could therefore face strong demand from different member states to support their efforts to promote democratic electoral processes, as well as for assistance on the legal, institutional, technical and administrative aspects of organizing and conducting elections, or to provide election observation and assessment.

To be able to respond adequately to this potential demand, the Arab League must implement a series of policy changes related to electoral assistance and election observation. In particular, the League needs to set up a clear legal and institutional framework to enable it to carry out election observation and election assistance in a coherent and comprehensive manner. It must devise a sound methodology and a code of conduct for its observers, defining the parameters, procedures and standards that apply to the entities providing electoral assistance. This framework should be in line with the Declaration of Principles for International Election Observation and the Code of Conduct for International Election Observers, both of which promote the impartiality and professionalism of election observers.

The Arab League needs to develop overall consistency in the handling of requests from member states organizing elections or seeking assistance. An election observation and assistance unit is needed to provide adequate support, evaluate requests for electoral assistance, formulate policy and guidelines on electoral matters, undertake assessment missions, and maintain contacts with regional and other intergovernmental organizations to ensure appropriate joint working arrangements and prepare joint EOMs and assistance.

In addition, for the Arab League to play an important role in this field will require adequate levels of funding. The League should also create and maintain a roster of electoral experts, on which its EOMs can count to provide qualified technical consultants for its observation missions.

Finally, the Arab League should be guided in its election observation and election assistance work by the electoral cycle approach, which implies moving away from election day assistance towards more medium- and long-term intervention. Activities intended to provide Arab countries with electoral assistance or to observe elections must be planned in this light in order to ensure a positive impact for the Arab League's efforts in the field of elections.

Conclusions

The Arab League has to date played an important and positive role in both election assistance and election observation. However, its efforts remain modest and are far from meeting the needs of its member states in terms of reform and assistance.

In the light of the important momentum for reform in the Arab region, the Arab League needs to respond positively to the requests for assistance that will come from its democratizing member states. In order to meet these requests, the League will need to undertake a comprehensive policy reform, set up a clear institutional and legal framework for election observation and election assistance, and put in place a more effective mechanism for the mobilization of resources and funding. The League will need to move away from ad hoc interventions to a standardized methodology and the adoption of a code of conduct. The recommendations made above will enable the League to comply with international best practices and become the key player in election observation and election assistance in the Arab region.

Selected bibliography

Barnett, Michael N., 'Sovereignty, Nationalism and Regional Order in the Arab States System', *International Organization*, 49/3 (Summer 1995), pp. 479–510

Brumberg, Daniel, 'Democratization in the Arab World? The Trap of Liberalized Autocracy', *Journal of Democracy*, 13/4 (October 2002), pp. 56–68

Carapico, Sheila, *International Elections Experts, Monitors and Representations in the Arab World*, EUI Working Papers, RSCAS 2008/24, Mediterranean Programme Series, European University Institute, Florence (2008), available at <http://www.eui.eu>

Carothers, Thomas and Ottaway, Marina, *Uncharted Journey: Promoting Democracy in the Middle East* (Washington, DC: Carnegie Endowment, 2005)

Commission of the European Communities, Communication on EU Election Assistance and Observation (Brussels, 11 April 2000), COM(2000) 191

Goodwin-Gill, Guy S., *Free and Fair Elections* (Geneva: Inter-Parliamentary Union, 2006)

Herb, Michael, 'Princes and Parliaments in the Arab World', *Middle East Journal*, 58/3 (Summer 2004), pp. 367–84

Human Rights Watch, *Algeria: Elections in the Shadow of Violence and Repression* (Washington, DC: Human Rights Watch, 1997), available at <http://www.hrw.org>

Huntington, Samuel P., *The Third Wave: Democratization in the Late Twentieth Century* (Norman: University of Oklahoma Press, 1991)

IOF, *Rapport de la mission d'observation: élections présidentielles de Djibouti du 9 avril 1999* [Observation mission report: Djibouti presidential elections of 9 April 1999], available at <http://www.francophonie.org>

Meital, Yoram, 'The Struggle over Political Order in Egypt: The 2005 Elections', *Middle East Journal*, 60/2 (Spring 2006), pp. 257–79

Al-Midani, Mohammed Amin and Cabanettes, Mathilde, 'The Arab Charter of Human Rights', *Boston University International Law Journal*, 24 (2006)

Pact of the League of Arab States, *Arab Law Quarterly*, 7/2 (1992), pp. 148–52

Posusney, Marsha Pripstein, 'Multi-Party Elections in the Arab World: Institutional Engineering and Oppositional Strategies', *Studies in Comparative International Development*, 36/4 (Winter 2002), pp. 34–62

Rishmawi, Mervat, 'The Arab Charter on Human Rights and the League of Arab States: An Update', *Human Rights Law Review*, 10/1 (2010)

Roberts, Hugh, 'Algeria's Contested Elections', *Middle East Report* (1998), pp. 21–24

Sadiki, Larbi, *Rethinking Arab Democratization: Elections without Democracy* (Oxford: Oxford University Press, 2009)

Salem, Elie A., 'Arab Nationalism: A Reappraisal', *International Journal*, 17/3 (Summer 1962), pp. 289–99

Schedler, Andreas, 'The Nested Game of Democratization by Elections', *International Political Science Review*, 23/1 (2002), pp. 103–22

Seabury, Paul, 'The League of Arab States: Debacle of a Regional Arrangement', *International Organization*, 3/4 (November 1949), pp. 633–42

UNDP and AFESD, *Arab Human Development, Arab Human Development Report 2002: Creating Opportunities for Future Generations* (Amman: United Nations Publications, 2002)

Whitehead, Laurence, Democratization: *Theory and Experience* (Oxford: Oxford University Press, 2002)

Notes

[1] The current members of the League of Arab States are Algeria, Bahrain, Comoros, Djibouti, Egypt, Iraq, Jordan, Kuwait, Lebanon, Libya, Mauritania, Morocco, Oman, Palestine, Qatar, Saudi Arabia, Somalia, Sudan, Syria, Tunisia, the United Arab Emirates and Yemen.

[2] Cf. Droz-Vincent, Philippe, 'Quel avenir pour l'autoritarisme dans le monde arabe?', *Revue Française de Science Politique*, 54/6 (2004), pp. 945–79; Huntington, Samuel P., 'The Clash of Civilizations?', *Foreign Affairs*, 72/3 (Summer 1993), pp. 22–49; and Takeyh, Ray, 'Faith-Based Initiatives [Can Islam bring democracy to the Middle East?]', *Foreign Policy*, 127 (December/November 2001), pp. 68–70.

[3] Among other initiatives see the Broader Middle East and North Africa Initiative, a multilateral development and reform plan aimed at fostering economic and political liberalization in a wide geographic area of Arab and non-Arab Muslim countries, launched during the G8 Meeting in 2004.

[4] League of Arab States Council Resolution No. 6302, 24 March 2003.

[5] The missions led by Nabila Abdelkader Goddi, the Arab League's senior elections expert, to Comoros and Djibouti confirm this. The statements published at the end of the missions reflected a high degree of professionalism and objectivity.

[6] Libya collaborated in these missions even though the Libyan people were totally denied the fundamental right to elect and choose their own rulers.

[7] In addition, some authors and organizations have accused the Arab League of complicity because of its failure to report on the serious human rights violations during the 1995 presidential elections in Algeria (Human Rights Watch 1997; Roberts 1998).

Chapter 5

The Responsibility to Expose: The Role of OAS Electoral Observation Missions in the Promotion of the Political Rights of Women

Chapter 5

Betilde Muñoz-Pogossian

The Responsibility to Expose: The Role of OAS Electoral Observation Missions in the Promotion of the Political Rights of Women[1]

Introduction

Since 2006, the Organization of American States (OAS) has taken significant steps to professionalize and systematize the monitoring of electoral processes in the Americas. To this end, the OAS has created tools to standardize the observation process through quantitative and qualitative inputs that provide the basis for an overall assessment of elections. This standardization process has been vital to steering OAS electoral observation missions (EOMs) towards a 'third generation' of electoral observation, that is, long-term, comprehensive missions that focus on the overall quality of an electoral process from a wider perspective (Spehar and Muñoz-Pogossian 2007), as opposed to limiting observation to the day of the election. In this context, it was important for the OAS, as the leading intergovernmental regional organization monitoring elections in the Americas, to take the lead in mainstreaming a gender perspective into its election observation methodology.

Other organizations that observe elections in the Western hemisphere do not systematically factor in the issue of gender as a key component of their assessments of electoral processes. At the Third International Meeting on the Implementation of the Declaration of Principles for International Election Observation, held in Maputo in 2008, the international organizations that monitor elections in the Americas, including the National Democratic Institute, the European Union, the Carter Center and the OAS, noted that, although mandates and commitments exist at the higher institutional level to consider gender issues in their work, there is a palpable reluctance to spend time and resources on the issue, as well as an overall lack of political will to follow up on promises to do so.

Thus, the mechanisms within these organizations that promote and defend democracy do not systematically take into account a basic underlying aspect of every definition of democracy: the equal participation of women and men in the political process. The fact that the OAS, as well as other organizations that monitor elections in the region, observes elections without systematically taking a gender perspective into account ultimately means that they are unable to identify areas in which shortcomings persist. As a result, these deficiencies in the equal participation of women and men in the political-electoral process are perpetuated. This leads to an ongoing endorsement of elections in the Americas as 'democratic', in spite of the persistent underrepresentation of women in the democratic institutions and processes of the region.

In the light of the above, an institutional decision was taken at the OAS to design a standardized methodology that incorporates a gender perspective into its election observation efforts. This methodology allows the OAS to assess, as well as contribute to, the full and equal participation of women and men in the electoral process at all levels—as voters, as candidates in national and local elections, as leaders of state institutions (Cabinet members), in electoral management bodies (EMBs) and in political party structures—with the overall objective of identifying and exposing the barriers that still exist to full political participation in a given country, within the context of the electoral process observed.

Making women's participation in the electoral process visible: a theoretical framework

An international election observation is a process in which an organized group of individuals from outside the host country systematically carries out a series of complex actions and activities to observe an electoral process in a direct, complete and precise manner (OAS 2010: 10). EOMs are a mechanism used by the OAS to help strengthen representative democracy in the Americas and promote the political rights of citizens in the context of electoral processes. In general, observation covers all three phases of an electoral process: the pre-electoral phase, beginning with the calling of elections and ending with the electoral silence prior to polling day; the day of the election; and the post-electoral phase, which culminates in the official proclamation of results.[2] The observation experience of the OAS has demonstrated that the pre-electoral phase is when the most significant concerns tend to arise, especially issues related to equity in electoral competition.

As a response to this reality, the OAS has been developing methodologies that will provide its EOMs with the tools to conduct rigorous and systematic analyses of electoral competition focused on the concept of equity. In the electoral context, equity is defined as the existence, in all three phases of the electoral process, of conditions that ensure that all voters are able to exercise their franchise and all candidates are able to participate on a level playing field in the competition for public office. The observation of conditions of equity in electoral competition necessarily involves paying close attention to whether such conditions hold in the exercise of political rights. From the perspective of gender equality, electoral equity is understood as the existence of conditions in which women and men are able to exercise their rights of political citizenship in an equal manner. Political citizenship is exercised in the three substantial manifestations of these rights: the right to elect and to be elected; the right to participate in the management of public affairs and the formulation of public policy; and the right of access to public service, that is, the right to hold political office (Bareiro and Torres 2009: 30).

Gender equality in the Americas

In the Americas, the region in which OAS EOMs are deployed, various obstacles stand in the way of gender equality in the exercise of political rights. These barriers, although different in different contexts, are largely a consequence of the social roles assigned to men and women—roles that have both cultural and historical origins. It is essential to bring to light the structural conditions, practices, policies and other elements that prevent women from the full exercise of their political citizenship. Exposing these obstacles will allow OAS EOMs to formulate targeted recommendations to help and encourage member states to overcome this democratic deficit.

A historical reflection on the political rights of women reveals that, in spite of the many advances achieved in this area, the equal representation of women in all aspects of public life remains an unfulfilled objective. Persistent inequality is borne out in statistics on political participation. In Latin America, for example, on average women represent 50 per cent of the electorate, but only occupy an average of 21 per cent of the seats in Congress and 22 per cent of Cabinet positions. Female representation in electoral bodies is also limited. In 2011, women held 22 per cent of such positions, while an even smaller percentage were in charge of these bodies. In the 35 OAS member states, only five women currently serve as head of government: Cristina Fernández in Argentina, Laura Chinchilla in Costa Rica, Dilma Rousseff in Brazil, Portia Simpson-Miller in Jamaica and Kamla Persad-Bissessar in Trinidad and Tobago. Low levels of representation are also found at the municipal level, refuting the common assumption that there is a higher level of involvement by women in issues that directly affect them and their families. On average, only 20.7 per cent of town/city councillors in Latin America are women. The situation is worse at the mayoral level: only 7.9 per cent of Latin American mayors were women in 2009.[3]

There are numerous explanations for the disproportionately small percentage of women in public life. In addition to entrenched cultural barriers, female aspirants to political office are hampered by inequalities in media coverage, differentiated access to campaign finance, resistance by party elites and political harassment, to name a few. The latter problem is exemplified by the infamous case of the 'Juanitas'[4] in Mexico, in which victorious women candidates resigned immediately before taking office to be replaced by their male substitutes. Furthermore, the reality of these numbers is reflected in the short-sighted practices and outlooks of state decision-making bodies. Political decisions should benefit all members of society, but 'the extent to which these bodies take into account the experience of a broad spectrum of society will indicate the degree to which those decisions are adequate and whether they tackle the necessities of society as a whole, and not simply those of one or several groups in particular' (Ginwala 2002).[5] As a result, the absence of women in decision-making positions is reflected in political agendas that fail to address the issues that affect women in particular. Public policies are rarely considered from a gender perspective. The consequence is a negative feedback loop, in which the very lack of female representation in decision-making bodies becomes an obstacle to any systemic change, thus perpetuating the status quo.

The role of the OAS

It is here that OAS EOMs, by exposing the obstacles to both electoral participation and political representation, can play a fundamental role in the quest for more equitable societies. Adopting the logic of the principle of the Responsibility to Protect (RtP),[6] the OAS, as a multilateral body and representing its member states, undoubtedly has the 'responsibility to expose'. In other words, it is a duty of the OAS to support its member states in their obligation to protect and promote the rights of their citizens: in this case, women. This vision of the mandate for electoral observation does not infringe on the sovereignty or equality of states, but rather aims to promote respect for the universal standards that underlie and underpin human rights; standards which are supported by international law and endorsed by the states themselves. As a multilateral body, the OAS is tasked with helping states to comply with their obligations as well as ensuring that they do so in a timely, decisive and preventative manner, and trying to identify—by means of concrete recommendations from its EOMs—mechanisms to promote the full exercise of the political rights of women.

How can the OAS use its electoral observation mandate to contribute to making women more visible? Incorporating a gender perspective into electoral observation goes beyond numbers. In other words, it is not sufficient to ensure gender balance and the equal representation of both sexes in the composition of missions, although this is a necessary step (as well as the policy of the OAS Department of Electoral Cooperation and Observation (DECO) and the OAS as a whole).[7] Figure 5.1 summarizes the percentage of women in the teams deployed to the observed country during an OAS EOM, including mission leadership, the core group, regional coordinators and international observers. Gender-focused electoral observation has to go beyond this to identify, describe and analyse the causes of those inequalities that affect the political rights of women in an electoral context.

Figure 5.1 Participation by women in OAS electoral observation missions

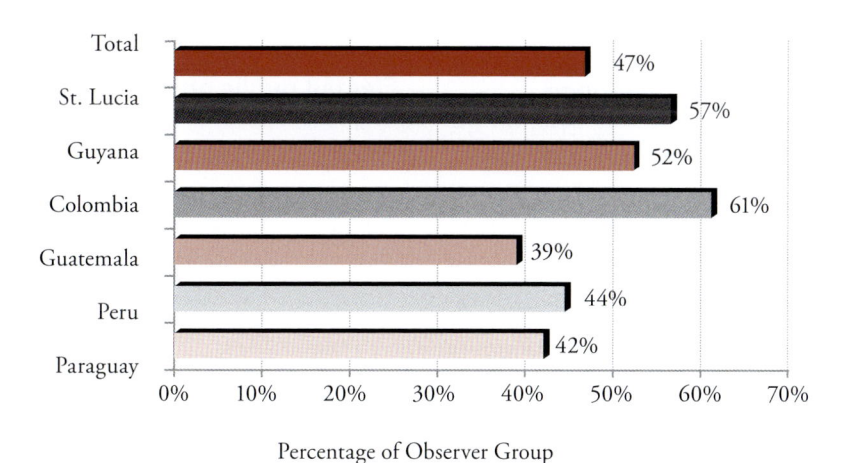

Country	Percentage
Total	47%
St. Lucia	57%
Guyana	52%
Colombia	61%
Guatemala	39%
Peru	44%
Paraguay	42%

Percentage of Observer Group

Source: OAS/DECO – chart created for this chapter.

Focusing on the OAS definition of democratic elections, OAS EOMs assess the conditions for the exercise of women's political rights from four perspectives. The first is that the elections are inclusive, in that all citizens—both male and female—enjoy conditions that allow them to exercise their right to vote and are effectively trained to exercise this right. The second is that the elections are clean, in the sense that the electoral preferences of both male and female voters are respected and faithfully recorded. The third is that elections are competitive, in that diverse options are offered to the electorate and both male and female candidates can participate in conditions of relative equality. Finally, the fourth perspective is that the main public offices are filled through regular elections, and that those elected are not removed once in power. Based on the attributes of democratic elections, DECO has systematically identified quantitative and qualitative indicators to assess gender equality in every aspect of the observed electoral process from registration and polling station access to the freedom of association and the right to access to information. The four axes of the OAS definition of democratic election are explained below, in Figure 5.2

Figure 5.2 The concept of democratic elections

Inclusive elections: Are all citizens sufficiently prepared to express their preferences in elections? ✓ Universal and equitable suffrage ✓ Effective exercise of the right to vote	Clean elections: Are all voters' preferences respected and accurately recorded? ✓ Integrity of voters' preferences ✓ Precise recording of voters' preferences
Competitive elections: Are voters able to choose impartially among candidates? ✓ Right to stand for public office ✓ Basic guarantees for electoral campaign	Elected public office: Are public offices filled through periodic elections? ✓ Periodic elections for top national offices ✓ Irreversibility of elections results

Source: OAS/DECO – table created for training of international observers.

Thus, OAS EOMs are ideally suited to assess the gap between formal equality and actual equality, and to expose the disparities between the rights and guarantees enshrined in international treaties and a reality in which women still confront a series of barriers impeding their ability to vote, and in which, in many cases, women do not enjoy equal opportunities to compete for public office.

In addition, the inclusion of this gender focus entails substantive benefits to the work of strengthening democracy carried out by the OAS through its EOMs. The most significant of these benefits is the possibility that the conclusions and recommendations formulated by the OAS in its observation missions and presented to the governments and electoral authorities of the host country will serve as springboards for change. Ideally, recommendations should result in technical cooperation projects directed at strengthening the capacity of electoral authorities to promote gender equality. More generally, they provide the impetus for OAS member states to initiate or strengthen processes to transform the asymmetrical relationship between men and women in the political-electoral arena. After all, the underlying goal of this observation methodology is to find solutions to one of the biggest problems facing democracy in the Latin American and Caribbean region: gender inequality.

The methodology at work: beyond the theoretical framework

In order to ground this theoretical vision in practice and to determine exactly how it should be implemented within the framework of an OAS EOM, the methodology was tested in various electoral processes in 2010 and 2011. Pilots were carried out during the municipal elections in Paraguay (November 2010), the presidential elections in Peru (April 2011), the presidential elections in Guatemala (September 2011), the municipal elections in Colombia (October 2011) and the general election in Guyana (November 2011). The experiences of the observation team deployed for the Saint Lucia general election in November 2011 are also included below. Given the diversity of political contexts and types of elections observed, each mission presented distinct challenges. Each shed new light on the best ways to practically apply gender observation methodology in the context of an OAS EOM, and revealed recurring themes and challenges to the full exercise of political rights by women.

Paraguay

The OAS brought together a team composed of a DECO specialist and two gender experts from the International Institute for Democracy and Electoral Assistance (International IDEA) (a Gender Analysis Team) to conduct the first pilot of the observation methodology during the 2010 municipal elections in Paraguay. As a signatory to the major international legal instruments on gender equality, and a country with constitutional guarantees on equal political rights for men and women as well as a quota,[8] Paraguay was an ideal case in which to test the gaps between norms and practice. Despite Paraguay's favourable legal environment, the EOM's analysis of candidate lists revealed a low percentage of women candidates (9.6%). Women were often placed towards the bottom of the lists. In the context of Paraguay's closed list electoral system,[9] this low placement severely jeopardized the electability of women candidates. Even considering that its threshold of 20 per cent is the lowest in the region, the quota proved ineffective in its avowed aim of increasing the political participation of women. Interviews with stakeholders led the EOM to conclude that the quota is ineffective for several reasons: it is only applied to primary elections, i.e. internal elections within political parties to select candidates; it lacks adequate mechanisms to force compliance; and there is a lack of political will within political parties to include women at the top of their lists. During the EOM in Paraguay, the team first encountered an obstacle that was to be a common feature in the countries of the region: a lack of available electoral information disaggregated by sex. In this case, information gaps prevented the team from verifying the total percentage of women candidates at the national level—a vital data point.

The Gender Analysis Team gathered information on the voting process by incorporating gender-specific questions into the standard questionnaires completed by the international observers. This tool gave the EOM critical and unprecedented amounts of data on the gender make-up of poll workers, as well as the percentage of women serving as presidents, party agents and domestic observers (see Table 5.1). Observer testimony also revealed that there was a high proportion of women performing all of these functions.

The discrepancy between the high number of women participating in the administration of the electoral process and the low numbers of women candidates and women in positions of authority unfortunately proved to be a recurring theme in the region. In Paraguay, observers noted that this tendency is reflective of the 'secretarial' conception held by political parties of the role of women in the political process. The obstacles presented by entrenched cultural norms proved to be an important explanation for gender inequality in Paraguay. Incorporating gender perspectives into state and electoral bodies was identified by the EOM as one possible way forward. In this sense, the establishment of a specialist Gender Unit within the Paraguayan Electoral Justice Tribunal represents a promising development, one that will hopefully lead to an increased focus on the promotion of women's political participation and training.[10]

Peru

As was the case in Paraguay, the team conducting the gender pilot in the Peruvian presidential elections consisted of DECO gender specialists and gender experts from International IDEA who were contracted to help design the methodology. As a result of this pilot, it was decided that in future the gender methodology will be implemented largely by an EOM core group, with the help of a gender specialist responsible for training observers, conducting interviews and compiling the information gathered. The idea is that a gender perspective will thus be 'mainstreamed' and incorporated into every aspect of an EOM's work.

The team in Peru found that, as might be expected, the passage of a gender quota in 1997 had contributed to a notable increase in the political participation of women at the legislative level. The percentage of women candidates running for Congress rose from 11.3 per cent in 1995 to 40 per cent in 2011. Not only did more women candidates appear on the ballot paper, but the electorate was increasingly predisposed to vote for women when they were given a chance to rank their preferences at the ballot box. Nonetheless, analysis of candidate lists revealed persistent gaps between men and women. Despite the strong performance of women candidates at the polls—Peru is among the countries with the most women legislators—women rarely appear at the top of the lists put forward by political organizations. The EOM learned that political parties still tend to view men as 'winners' and still tend to place male candidates in the key electable positions.

Another obstacle for women candidates in the Peruvian elections, also identified in Paraguay, was unequal access to political finance. Resource disparities between women and men are especially important in the context of the Peruvian electoral system. With preferential voting,[11] electoral performance depends to a large degree on the amount of money spent in the media and other types of publicity. Given the discrepancies in salary between men and women in Peru, the EOM recommended the implementation of gender-focused public financing to level the playing field for women candidates. In general, the Peruvian elections exposed an important truth: a quota is not a panacea. Merely stipulating a quota for women on candidate lists does not by itself translate into equal opportunity or gender parity. The Peruvian pilot proved that equity in the political system must go beyond compliance with formal regulations. It involves imbuing the system and the political actors involved with a gender perspective and a substantive commitment to gender equality in political participation.

Guatemala

By the time of the third pilot, the presidential elections in Guatemala in September 2011, the gender observation methodology had largely been defined and the gender analysis team was reduced to two DECO specialists—one female and one male. Findings from the Guatemala EOM revealed significant progress in an area that, despite its fundamental importance to the political participation of women, is often overlooked: voter registration. The fact that women constituted a majority on the electoral register for the first time represents a historic achievement for Guatemala, especially in the light of the fact that women make up 52 per cent of the Guatemalan population. Unfortunately, the increased number of women registered to vote was not reflected in greater female participation in the electoral competition. Less than 15 per cent of the nominated candidates were women. Female participation was even lower at the local level, where only 6 per cent of the nearly 2500 mayoral candidates were women.

The 2011 Guatemalan elections exemplified the important role played by political parties as the bodies responsible for deciding which candidates are presented to the electorate. The combination of a lack of internal democracy within political parties, a closed list electoral system in which voters cannot express their preferences for individual candidates, and the rising cost of electoral campaigns (in which the candidates themselves are often responsible for their own fundraising) makes for an unfavourable climate for the participation of women. This is reflected in the 12 per cent figure of women actually elected to serve in Congress in 2011, the extremely low percentage of women mayors (2.1%) and the stubbornly small presence of women in Guatemalan politics since democracy was restored in 1985. As a result, the OAS EOM recommended that serious consideration should be given to adopting the comprehensive affirmative action measure proposed by several political parties and civil society groups that was then being debated in the legislature.[12]

Women represented a majority of poll workers in the election, but were not assigned leading roles in the administration of polling stations. Their participation as party agents and domestic observers was less significant (see Table 5.1).

However, one positive aspect observed during the Guatemalan elections was the presence of women in positions of authority within the EMB. Three of the five magistrates on the Supreme Electoral Tribunal, including the President, were women. This is an interesting point given data that indicate that, as of

2012, only 22 per cent of the region's EMBs are led by women. Largely as a result of female representation on the leadership of the Tribunal, gender issues have begun to be placed on the administrative agenda, as evidenced by the dissemination of gender-sensitive training materials and the creation of a unit dedicated to political training and the promotion of the political participation of women. As these groups have only recently been formed, their effect on the political landscape in either the short or the long term cannot be determined. However, the importance attached to such issues by the supreme electoral authority must certainly be interpreted as progress. In its final report, the EOM commended the work of the units within the Supreme Electoral Tribunal dedicated to political training for women, and recommended compliance with legislation that stipulates that the staffing of regional electoral bodies take gender into account.

Colombia

The OAS had an opportunity to send a gender observation team to the October 2011 municipal elections in Colombia, in which a gender quota was in effect for the first time. The measure, passed in December 2010, obliges parties to grant at least 30 per cent of the places on the candidate lists for municipal councils, municipal assemblies and national Congress to women. Prior to the 2011 elections, the country had experienced stagnation in terms of the number of women serving as members of Congress. Female representation was even lower at the municipal and mayoral levels: only 3 per cent of governors were women. The EOM was pleased to note that the application of the quota was instrumental to increasing the percentage of women candidates from 19.6 per cent in the 2007 municipal elections to 35.2 per cent in the 2011 electoral process.

That participation by women exceeded the baseline stipulated in the quota is a sign of optimism for the future of gender equality in Colombia. Furthermore, the EOM was encouraged by the fact that the quota law also instituted more substantive affirmative action measures: an obligation to incorporate gender equity in candidate selection into political party statutes; and public financing incentives for parties linked to the number of women elected to public councils. In the light of legislative efforts to repeal certain parts of the bill, the EOM recommended that the Colombian government continue its efforts to promote the political participation of women and to train women at all levels of the political process.

Guyana

Because OAS EOMs are deployed to the Caribbean as well as Latin America, and in the light of the inherent political and social differences between the two regions, pilot projects were carried out in both regions. The Guyana general election in November 2011 provided the venue for the first OAS gender observation in a Caribbean country. Guyana is the only country in the Caribbean with a gender quota for party lists, a policy instituted in 2000. Women made up almost 40 per cent of the candidates in 2011. The stipulation that a minimum of one-third of all candidates must be female has coincided with significant progress towards gender equality in political participation over the past two decades. In 1992, 12 of the 70 members of the National Assembly were women, or 18.5 per cent. Following the 2011 elections, the number of women lawmakers had grown to 21, representing 30 per cent of the total. Guyana currently ranks 25th in the world in terms of the percentage of women in the legislature.

Although the implementation of the quota must be considered a significant step forward in the promotion of women's participation in politics, Guyana's electoral system grants party leaders complete discretion in deciding which candidates from the list gain seats in the assembly. Such a system makes the number of women candidates on an electoral list virtually irrelevant and severely weakens the effectiveness of the quota. The OAS EOM noted with concern that in the 2011 election, only one of the four major political parties fielded a woman at the top of its list. Furthermore, female representation at the upper levels of electoral administration was minimal. All seven commissioners on the Guyana Elections Commission were male, but over 75 per cent of the poll workers at observed polling stations were women (see Table 5.1). The EOM therefore recommended that the Guyanese government show increased commitment to issues of importance to women by working closely with political parties to implement effective measures to ensure that women candidates are guaranteed fair representation among those designated by the party to serve in the national assembly. The mission also recommended that the government strengthen its efforts, in cooperation with civil society, to promote training programmes for women candidates and to enact legislation that proactively promotes gender equality in all spheres of life in Guyana.

Mainstreamed perspective in OAS EOMs: the example of Saint Lucia

The process of gender mainstreaming is having unintended, albeit positive, effects. The OAS did not formally carry out an implementation of the methodology during the Saint Lucian general elections in November 2011, but 'gender lenses' were used to observe the same issues covered by the OAS in every EOM. Issues of registration, political financing and the nomination of candidates, among others, were seen from a perspective that seeks to expose differences in the exercise of political rights by men and women. The standardized questionnaire was used to collect gender-disaggregated data. The mission noted that all observed polling stations were staffed with the designated polling officials, 87 per cent of whom were women. Sixty per cent of alternate polling officials were women. Among the presiding officers, 80 per cent were women (see Table 5.1).

The evidence suggests that women face challenges in fully exercising their political rights in Saint Lucia. Women made up the majority of poll workers, with an average of 87 per cent participation in the polling sites observed by the OAS. The majority of party agents were also women. Nonetheless, the number of female candidates remained limited. The EOM recognized the progress made in increasing the percentage of female candidacies from 8.3 per cent in the 2006 election to 10 out of 52 candidates or 19 per cent in 2011, but there is still much to be done. In terms of political office, only two of the four women contesting the general election for the opposition party won seats. Each won a closely fought election by a single-digit vote margin. In the case of the government party, two women contested the election but only one won a seat. Therefore, the St Lucian parliament will now have only 17 per cent female representation. Based on these results, the EOM recommended that efforts should be made to ensure that the active participation of women as voters, polling clerks and party agents is also reflected in the lists of candidates.

It was recommended that Saint Lucians promote a serious discussion on the role of women in politics—and specifically whether there is a need for a quota system to provide incentives for women party activists—and on how political parties can encourage their political leadership.

Conclusions

A number of specific conclusions emerged from this limited implementation of the methodology to incorporate a gender perspective into OAS EOMs. These lessons will serve as guidelines for determining which aspects merit the most emphasis in order to achieve a gender observation that is both comprehensive and effective in its aim of promoting equity in electoral competition.

First, the low levels of female political representation, particularly in high-level positions, are a consequence of the hierarchical organization of political parties. The ability of women to occupy senior positions relates to the nature of the recruitment processes for party leaderships and the way in which party leaders are nominated or elected. Given that political parties are the organizations exclusively responsible for presenting candidates to the electorate, they effectively serve as gatekeepers to political office. It is therefore fundamental to observe how women are represented in leadership positions within parties. Through the implementation of this methodology, the OAS has been able to document that women participate actively as party members and activists, even making up a majority of the agents or poll-watchers employed by political organizations during elections. The data gleaned from the OAS pilots, derived from questionnaires completed by international observers, are summarized in Table 5.1.

Table 5.1 Women's participation in elections in Latin America: a comparative overview

	Polling stations	Polling station presidents	Party agents	Domestic observers	Legislative candidates
PARAGUAY					
Women	54.2%	57.1%	54.6%	72.2%	9.6%
PERU					
Women	45%	40%	52%	58%	39.4%
GUATEMALA					
Women	54%	36%	40%	36%	24%
GUYANA					
Women	83%	72%	72%	71%	31%
SAINT LUCIA					
Women	87%	80%	83%	100%	17%

Note: In the case of Paraguay, the elections were municipal. Thus, the percentage of candidates in this case applies to positions in town councils.
Source: Data gathered by OAS EOMs, table created for this chapter.

The significant female involvement in the logistical and administrative aspects of the electoral process is not reflected in terms of candidacies. In the elections in which the OAS conducted pilots, the percentage of women included on legislative electoral lists averaged 26 per cent. In many cases the number was far lower. Even fewer were placed in electable positions within those lists, in most cases because of decisions made by party leaderships. This low percentage of women candidacies reflects the lack of political will on the part of political parties in the region to field women candidates or allow women to hold leadership positions. The evidence from the pilots clearly suggests that internal democracy within political parties leads to a more democratic political process at the national level, and thus greater opportunities for women to participate meaningfully in politics.

Second, female representation in key decision-making positions tends to increase when governments implement gender quotas, usually linked to the strategic objective identified in the 1995 Beijing Platform for Action of having women in 30 per cent of positions at decision-making levels. Within the region, only 13 countries (12 in Latin America and one in the Caribbean) have policies on quotas or gender parity for elections to the lower legislative chamber.[13] Five countries in the region have such policies for the upper legislative chamber.[14] Gender quotas have critics as well as advocates. Similarly, they have negative as well as positive qualities. Nonetheless, there is undeniable evidence that countries that have implemented some kind of affirmative action policy have presided over clear and in some cases significant advances towards greater representation of women in the political sphere. As a result, current debate in the region has shifted beyond quotas towards discussion of gender parity, and mechanisms to ensure that men and women assume equal representation in the different spheres of state administration. Ecuador, Bolivia and Costa Rica have moved in this direction through a series of legislative reforms.

Finally, affirmative action policies that focus on increasing access by women to political-electoral financing, when combined with the implementation of gender quotas, have demonstrably positive effects on the political participation of women. On the one hand, quotas ensure that women are placed on party lists. When designed effectively, such policies ensure that women are placed in winnable positions on these lists and therefore have a realistic chance of being elected. This correlation holds in spite of the fact that the candidate who spends more is not necessarily the one who ends up being elected. There are two distinct models of gender-focused public financing within the region. In the first model, the law requires political parties to dedicate a certain percentage of their permanent (non-electoral) public financing to the training of women. In Mexico, for example, each political party must annually set aside 2 per cent of its ordinary public financing for the training, promotion and political leadership development of women. Parties in Panama are obligated to devote 25 per cent of their public financing to training activities, of which 10 per cent must be directed to women, that is 2.5 per cent of the total. The second model requires parties to allot a given percentage of their total public financing to the training of women or to activities geared to increasing female political participation. In Brazil, for example, partisan organizations must designate a percentage, equal to at least 5 per cent of the total amount of public financing received, for the promotion and political participation of women. In Costa Rica, a specific law (Law Promoting the Social Equality of Women) stipulates that political parties are obliged to set aside a percentage of the public resources received to promote the training and political participation of women.[15] The opportunity to participate effectively in politics depends greatly on the capacity of candidates to obtain funds. When money is indispensable to a genuine possibility of winning an electoral race, difficulties in access to financing become an entry barrier that, by impeding the access of women to power, alters the balance of political representation and affects gender equality in democratic participation. Political financing is an issue that is fundamental to the effectiveness of the electoral system and the democratic process.

The incorporation of a gender perspective will allow OAS EOMs to bring to light concerns related to gender equity and women's political rights, and help place these issues on the political agenda. Making gender equity a focus of OAS EOMs will not only stimulate dialogue but also help identify new challenges and initiatives to strengthen the participation of women in political life. Failure to incorporate a gender focus, on the other hand, would simply reinforce existing conditions of inequality. Such inequitable conditions must be overcome in order to achieve a true democracy in which rights and freedoms are exercised fully by all people.[16] This makes the recommendations that emerge from EOMs fundamentally important. These recommendations, aimed at strengthening electoral processes and continually increasing their inclusivity, consolidate the impact of OAS EOMs as entities that are capable of transforming the current reality. While always respecting the sovereignty of states, the responsibility is, undoubtedly, to expose.

References

Bareiro, Line and Torres, Isabel, *Igualdad para una democracia incluyente* (San José: Inter-American Institute for Human Rights, 2009)

Congreso de la República de Guatemala, 'Initiative 4088' (August 2009), available at <http://200.12.63.122/archivos/iniciativas/registro4088.pdf>

Ginwala, Frene, 'Mujeres en el Parlamento: Más allá de los Números', Stockholm, International IDEA, 2002

Inter-American Commission of Women, 'OAS-Interamerican Commission of Women Plan of Action 2011–2016' (April 2011), available at <http://www.oas.org/en/cim/docs/CIM-StrategicPlan2011-2016-ENweb.pdf>

OAS, *Manual for OAS Observation Missions* (Washington, DC: General Secretariat of the OAS, 2010), available at <http://www.oas.org/en/spa/docs/Manual_Misiones_publicado_en.pdf>

Spehar, Elizabeth and Muñoz-Pogossian, Betilde with Raúl Alconada Sempé (eds), *The 2005–2006 Electoral Cycle in the Americas: A Review by the OAS General Secretariat* (Washington, DC: General Secretariat of the OAS, 2007)

Notes

[1] The author would like to thank the team members at the OAS Department for Electoral Cooperation and Observation, Tyler Finn and Sara Mía Noguera, for the research and editing support they provided in the preparation of this chapter.

[2] For more detailed information see the OAS *Manual for Electoral Observation Missions*.

[3] Data collected by International IDEA, available at <http://www.idea.int/vt/survey/by_gender.cfm>.

[4] The case of the Juanitas refers to eight deputies in Mexico who, after being elected in the 2009 legislative elections, requested leave on the first day of work as legislators so that the same number of men could take their seats. They were called 'juanitas' given the parallels with the case of Rafael Acosta, 'Juanito', a candidate for the Chief of the Iztapalapa Delegation in the municipal elections of the same year, who promised to resign so that a woman, Clara Brugada, could take that position.

[5] Author's translation.

[6] The RtP principle is a product of a report, *The Responsibility to Protect*, by the International Commission on Intervention and State Sovereignty of the United Nations. It proposes that the sovereignty of states entails not only a right to manage their internal affairs but also a primary responsibility to protect the population within its borders. The report also proposes that in the case of a state

that does not protect its population, due to a lack of either capacity or will, the responsibility then falls to the international community as a whole. The RtP principle is one of the most important normative advances in international law and is intended to ensure an effective response by the international community when confronted with the imminent risk of genocide or a similarly heinous crime, for example, the situation in Rwanda in 1994. Critics of the RtP principle argue that it opens the door to military intervention by the countries of the North in the countries of the South, where incidents of violence against the population are more likely to occur. The report of the Commission does not insist on military action, however, but instead takes a preventive stance on the issue, focusing on the strengthening of states' capacities to protect their populations. For more information see <http://web.idrc.ca/openebooks/960-7/>.

[7] For more information see OAS-Interamerican Commission of Women Plan of Action 2011–2016, <http://www.oas.org/en/cim/docs/CIM-StrategicPlan2011-2016-ENweb.pdf>.

[8] In the context of an electoral process, a gender quota is an affirmative action measure that stipulates that a certain percentage of the candidates fielded by a political party must be of a certain gender. For example, the electoral code in the Dominican Republic requires each party to put forward a minimum of 33% of women candidates.

[9] Under a proportional representation system, each party or political organization presents a list of candidates in a plurinominal electoral district. Electors vote for a party list and parties win seats in proportion to the percentage of the vote obtained. In closed-list systems, candidates are chosen according to the order in which they appear on the party list, a decision which is typically made by the party.

[10] Detailed information on the Gender Unit in the Electoral Justice Tribunal of Paraguay can be found at <http://www.tsje.gov.py/unidad-de-genero.php>.

[11] In a system of preferential or open-list voting, as in the case of Peru, electors can influence the order of candidates on lists by marking individual preferences on the ballot paper.

[12] This measure, Initiative 4088, which aims to reform Article 212 of the Law of Elections and Political Parties, would institute gender parity and alternability on candidate lists, and enforce sanctions for failure to comply with its requirements. More detailed information can be found at <http://200.12.63.122/archivos/iniciativas/registro4088.pdf>.

[13] In Latin America, Argentina, Bolivia, Brazil, Costa Rica, the Dominican Republic, Ecuador, Honduras, Mexico, Panama, Paraguay, Peru and Uruguay operate with quotas. Guyana is the only Caribbean country that has adopted a quota.

[14] In many cases, these quota laws establish a minimum percentage applicable to women or minimums/maximums that are applicable to both sexes. The legislation in Peru, for example, stipulates that men or women must make up at least 30% of candidates.

[15] Urizar, Alejandro and Noguera, Sara Mia, 'Working paper on Public Financing with a Gender Perspective', 2011 (unpublished).

[16] OAS, 'Manual for the Incorporation of the Gender Perspective into OAS Electoral Observation Missions', developed in collaboration with International IDEA (unpublished).

Chapter 6

Quality Management Systems and their Contribution to the Integrity of Elections

Chapter 6

María T. Mellenkamp and Pablo Gutiérrez

Quality Management Systems and their Contribution to the Integrity of Elections

Introduction

The Organization of American States (OAS) has been observing elections for longer than any other regional organization. Its experience working with its region's electoral management bodies (EMBs) leads it to assert that the magnitude and nature of the challenges faced by these institutions vary. In some countries these challenges might be considered basic or elementary, while in others, which have reached a higher level of institutional development, the challenges are more complex and abstract.

The challenges of electoral management are correlated to the general level of development in a country. Requests for technical support and cooperation have changed their nature. Although the OAS still provides technical cooperation on traditional topics, it is moving towards the implementation of solutions strictly oriented to improving confidence levels and professionalizing the region's EMBs. Needless to say, in order to receive this type of cooperation, EMBs must have achieved a level of maturity that enables them to make a qualitative leap in their structure and operations, and the way they relate to their 'clients'.

In the past decade, the OAS has started to look at new policy instruments aimed at building and strengthening the institutional capacities of the EMBs in the region. This new phase of cooperation is related to the implementation of quality management systems (QMS), which ends with the certification of processes or structures under the international standard ISO 9001. The advantages of introducing QMS into electoral bodies are innumerable: improved operational performance, reduced operating costs, increased reliability, better defined and documented procedures, increased employee awareness of quality and the development of a culture of continual improvement.

In the past four years, the OAS has provided technical cooperation in the QMS field to several countries in the region. The idea of implementing a tool traditionally used in the private arena in the public sector has provoked great interest among the region's EMBs. This resulted in the creation of a working group which is currently developing a new international standard for certifying elections. It focuses on seven processes: voter registration; registration of political organizations and candidates; electoral logistics and planning; vote casting; counting and the declaration of results; civic-electoral education; and the oversight of campaign financing.

Trust in an EMB's performance by citizens and political parties is vital not only for the success of the electoral process but also for the credibility of the newly elected government. The OAS Department for Electoral Cooperation and Observation (DECO) believes that the introduction of an innovative and technically feasible policy instrument such as the QMS is an effective and efficient way to address new challenges.

Democracy and elections are two inextricably linked concepts: one cannot occur successfully without the other. All democratic systems are supported through the holding of periodic elections, and elections cannot succeed within a political system other than democracy.

The purpose of this chapter is not to describe the status of democracy. The health of democracy depends on many diverse factors and, while acknowledging the important role of elections in every democracy, the focus of the chapter is on how to contribute to the consolidation of democracies by influencing electoral processes. In this regard, it is important that those responsible for organizing and managing electoral processes are able to ensure the integrity, transparency and fairness of elections.

The level of trust that political parties and citizens place in the electoral authority and its ability to carry out its organizational responsibilities is vital for both the credibility of the electoral processes and the reputation of the elected government.

EMBs, like other government institutions, are not immune from the trend for modernization and the search for new and better tools to improve governance, and are committed to a self-improvement process for organizing electoral processes. One such tool applicable to EMBs and other public or private institutions is the implementation of quality management systems and the certification of their processes under internationally recognized standards. Despite being a relatively new concept for the public sector and a tool originally formulated for the private sector, quality management is gaining popularity among government agencies and public bodies.

QMS when applied to electoral bodies (both those which organize elections and those with judicial functions in electoral matters) seek to preserve and strengthen institutions and to promote the professionalization, development and legitimacy of their actions. The application of quality management principles helps to improve the services provided to citizens and political organizations. Some electoral bodies in the region are demonstrating high levels of institutional growth and already taking a step towards quality.

Quality management systems

QMS are defined as a series of interconnected activities with the end goal of continually improving the effectiveness of an organization at managing production and/or providing services. By adhering to a QMS, an organization aims to comply with previously defined standards and customer expectations. Every QMS is supported by a documentation system that specifies responsibilities, procedures, inputs and outputs, and allows the organization to identify, monitor and measure its processes.

Regular and continued audits and certifications are conducted under a QMS to guarantee conformity to the standard and continual improvement in the performance of an organization. Certification is done against the ISO 9001:2008 norm. ISO 9001:2008 is the standard that provides **a set of standardized requirements for a quality management system,** regardless of what the user organization does, its size or whether it is in the private or public sector. It is the only ISO standard against which organizations can be certified—although **certification is not a compulsory requirement** of the standard.[1]

Certification under ISO quality management standards

The International Organization for Standardization (ISO) is a worldwide federation of national standards bodies. The organization has developed thousands of international standards on many subjects. One of these is ISO 9000, an integrated set of international standards and quality guidelines that have earned a worldwide reputation as a basis for establishing a QMS.

ISO 9001 falls within this set of standards. Over the years, QMS standards such as ISO 9001[2] have been successfully applied to different organizations to help improve their ability to increase customer satisfaction and meet statutory requirements, and to provide methods for establishing responsibilities in an organization, resource management, and service delivery and improvement.

Quality management principles

There are eight quality management principles on which the QMS standards of the ISO 9000 series are based:[3]

1) *Client orientation:* organizations should understand current and future customer needs, should meet customer requirements and should strive to exceed customer expectations.
2) *Leadership:* leaders establish unity of purpose and the direction of the organization. They should create and maintain an internal environment in which people can become fully involved in achieving the organization's objectives.
3) *Involvement of staff:* staff at all levels are the essence of an organization and their full involvement enables their abilities to be used for the organization's benefit.
4) *Process-based approach:* a desired result is achieved more efficiently when activities and related resources are managed as a process.
5) *Systems approach to management:* identifying, understanding and managing interrelated processes as a system contributes to the organization's effectiveness and efficiency in achieving its objectives.
6) *Continual improvement:* continual improvement of the organization's overall performance should be a permanent objective of the organization.
7) *Factual approach to decision making:* effective decisions are based on the analysis of data and information.
8) *Mutually beneficial supplier relationships:* an organization and its suppliers are interdependent and a mutually beneficial relationship enhances the ability of both to create value.

These principles can be used by senior management as a framework to guide their organizations towards performance improvement. They also serve as guides to understand the dynamics to be adopted by an institution that is to implement a QMS, as well as to determine the gaps in an institution at a given moment and the changes needed in order to comply with the ISO standard.

Certification process actors

Four types of organization form part of the certification process:

1) *Accreditation bodies:* specialized bodies that give formal recognition to certifying bodies regarding their competence to certify specific business sectors. At the same time, accreditation bodies supervise certification bodies, coordinate accreditation operations with government agencies, and promote the use of national accreditation systems.
2) *Certifying bodies:* independent, external bodies that certify that a product, process or service complies with the requirements specified in the applicable norms, laws and regulations.
3) *Consulting firms:* provide advisory services for the implementation of a QMS to those organizations which seek certification. Consulting firms design and implement strategies that contain the steps to be followed for the implementation of the QMS and subsequent certification.
4) *Organizations to be certified:* electoral bodies (in this case) that seek to be certified under ISO standards and are served either directly or indirectly by the organizations listed above.

Figure 6.1 describes, for example, the actors involved in the QMS implementation process and certification under ISO quality standards for the National Electoral Jury of Peru (Jurado Nacional de Elecciones de Perú, JNE).

Promoting electoral quality

Electoral administration and electoral justice are dynamic areas. Electoral competences are numerous and present diverse challenges that are renewed with each election.

The main advantages for the implementation of a QMS in an EMB are the optimization of electoral processes and procedures, the improvement of information management for the decision-making process, and achieving a change to an organizational culture of continual improvement.

Application of the principles of quality management aims to improve the service provided to the public and to political organizations. In this sense, the focus of quality management certification is not the certification itself, but putting public administration at the service of the citizenry. Quality management and certification are therefore means and not ends.

Quality management implies an institutional mindset that is open to change, and which enables and facilitates the incorporation of more efficient procedures and processes that can have an impact on citizens. DECO has witnessed the growth and evolution of EMBs in the region and has participated in the modernization of their electoral processes.

Figure 6.1 The actors involved in the QMS implementation process and certification under ISO quality standards for the Jurado Nacional de Elecciones de Perú

	Consulting Firm	Organization to Certify	Certifying entity	Accreditation entity	IATCA
Plan	DAEEL — Design a strategy for the implementation of the QMS of the organization, taking into consideration the processes to be included in the scope, and applicable legal and regulatory requirements.	JNE — Jurado Nacional de Elecciones, Garantía de la Voluntad Popular	SGS	UKAS QUALITY MANAGEMENT	IATCA
Do	Diagnose, train, implement, conduct follow ups and correct the strategy and its implementation	Actively work with the consultants executing the strategy for the implementation of a Management System, develop and comply with each of the requirements of administrative rules (i.e. quality)			
Check	Supports in receiving certification audits (not required in audits, but it is a good practice of consulting firms)	Receives Certification audits by the certifying entity	Conducts Certification audits .. Pre-Audit Audit Phase I (Documentation) Audit Phase II (Operational)		Accredits the competence of the auditors
Act	Support the organization addressing nonconformities (if any) to achieve a certificayion	Establishes plans of action and correct nonconformities (if any) to achieve a certification	Validate the corrections (If any)		
Results		SG of the Organization certified under the applicable international standard	Issue a certificate that the SG of the organization meets the standard of the applicable norms, statutory and policy requirements.	Credited: To the certifying organization (process audit) Endorse the certificate issued by the certification entity.	

Source: Department of Electoral Cooperation and Observation, Organization of American States.
Note: UKAS = United Kingdom Accreditation Service; IATCA = International Auditor and Training Certification Association, which has been replaced by IPC, the International Personnel Certification Association.

OAS electoral technical cooperation on QMS and ISO standards certification

The Department of Electoral Cooperation and Observation is in charge of developing and maintaining a permanent, professional electoral observation service, as well as providing technical assistance to OAS member states based on its ongoing efforts to improve procedures and practices in the field. DECO's mandate is specified in Chapter V, Article 23, of the Inter-American Democratic Charter, which establishes that 'member states, in the exercise of their sovereignty, may request that the Organization of American States provide advisory services or assistance for strengthening and developing their electoral institutions and processes, including sending preliminary missions for that purpose'.

Among DECO's main objectives are to improve the quality of services that EMBs provide to citizens and political organizations, and to strengthen their institutional capacity to hold elections that are inclusive, clean, competitive and periodic.

OAS methodology for the introduction of QMS and ISO certification for EMBs

Prior to the implementation of quality management standards projects, the OAS carries out a series of consultations with the relevant electoral bodies in order to design and define the scope of the project.

The OAS has developed an eight-stage standardized methodology for the implementation of QMS and the certification of EMBs. Each stage is implemented with the support of specialist technical staff.

1) *A diagnostic of key processes:* identification of sub-processes, activities and documentation, and a current index of the key processes. A sample and interviews are conducted to analyse the shortfalls and gaps between actual practice and ISO 9001:2008 requirements.
2) *Meeting with senior management:* a meeting to explain the role of the consulting firm that will carry out the implementation of a QMS, and the ways in which the QMS will improve the organization's performance.
3) *Training:* a series of activities for staff members to provide the necessary awareness, as well as basic and advanced knowledge of QMS and the areas involved in the project.
4) *Deployment, dissemination and alignment of strategic plans:* deployment

and alignment of strategic plans, timelines, implementation proposals and detailed work plans for closing gaps, including the definition of roles, conflict management, and the establishment of responsibilities for the project by staff, the organization and the work team.

5) *Design and structuring of the QMS:* conceptualization and design of the QMS according to each area or process, through the drafting of a preliminary Quality Manual outline which describes the structure of the QMS. Maps of key processes and their supporting processes are developed. The methodology is based on a systematic perspective that begins with the identification of macro-organizational processes. This perspective provides a global vision of the organization as well as the relationship between all the processes before reaching a greater level of detail in which these macro-processes are broken down into sub-processes and then into specific activities.

6) *Drafting and implementation of QMS documentation:* drafting and implementation of documents such as the Quality Manual, general and operational procedures, work plans and forms, as well as their oversight according to the requirements of ISO 9001:2008 and guidelines defined by the electoral body.

7) *Preliminary audit certification (conducted by the external certification body):* determination of findings in order to implement necessary modifications to carry out certification.

8) *Audit certification:* an audit that leads to the certification of the electoral body.

Figure 6.2 OAS Methodology stages

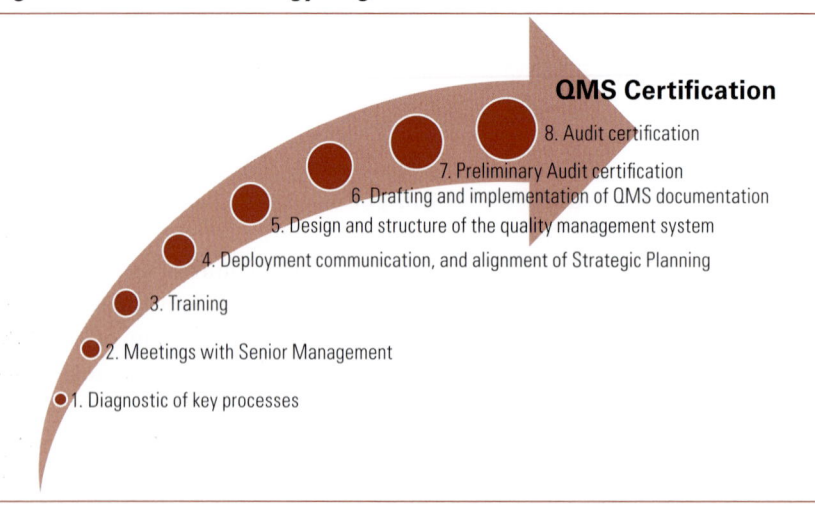

QMS Certification

8. Audit certification
7. Preliminary Audit certification
6. Drafting and implementation of QMS documentation
5. Design and structure of the quality management system
4. Deployment communication, and alignment of Strategic Planning
3. Training
2. Meetings with Senior Management
1. Diagnostic of key processes

Source: Department of Electoral Cooperation and Observation, Organization of American States.

Implementation of a QMS is likely to achieve results in a shorter period of time in those EMBs in which procedures are documented and staff are well trained. In this sense, although there are different levels of development across EMBs, they all have the sovereignty to define their own structures and the manner in which they carry out electoral processes. After all, the common goal of all electoral bodies is to organize free and transparent elections.

Country cases

To date, the OAS has provided technical cooperation to the EMBs of Panama and Peru to implement a QMS and certification under ISO quality standards. In these cases, all eight stages of the OAS methodology were implemented, resulting in the certification of the electoral body. The OAS has also provided technical cooperation to the EMB in Costa Rica through a diagnostic of some of the organization's key processes.

The Panamanian certification

In order to strengthen transparency in its processes, in 2006 the Electoral Tribunal of Panama, the sole EMB in the country, requested OAS technical cooperation with the implementation of a QMS and ISO 9001 certification. The OAS secured financial support to implement the project, which started with project design in 2006 and ended in May 2010 when the Electoral Tribunal was certified.

The project positioned the Electoral Tribunal of Panama as the first EMB in the region to reach the goal of achieving certification.

The scope of the certification covered three key departments: the Department of the Civil Registry, the Identification Card Department and the Department of Electoral Organization; and one support department, the Information Technology Department. Key processes within each department were subject to certification.

The process of QMS certification was conducted under a 'multi-site quality management system'. This type of system aims to determine the level of compliance with the norm by means of a non-statistical sample of the records required by both the standard and the management system in effect. The goal is to identify evidence of procedural oversight, compliance with norms and continual improvement.

During the implementation of the project, the design and structure of the QMS was elaborated for each of the departments and their processes, taking into consideration supporting processes and establishing minimum requirements for each process (process mapping). The responsibilities and functions of the staff within the departments were also defined, as well as the degree of interaction between the different departments. Four quality manuals were drafted, one for each department. As a result, the Electoral Tribunal now has better defined and regulated processes and procedures in all four departments. The Electoral Tribunal now has over 60 documented procedures, which are constantly updated and posted on its intranet site: 'Best practices portal for the use of the staff'.

Staff members at all levels were trained in QMS topics in order to facilitate the implementation and sustainability of the project. A total of 100 training sessions were carried out and more than 1000 staff members were trained.

QMS implementation and ISO certification achieved tangible results for the Electoral Tribunal of Panama:

- a 15 per cent increase in effectiveness in the issuance of certificates in the civil registry;
- a 10 per cent improvement in updating citizens' address information between the first quarter of 2010 and the second quarter of 2011; and
- between January and September 2011, 99.86 per cent of technology-related incidents were resolved.

The Tribunal now provides a citizen-focused service which is evaluated by opinion polls of the population. The QMS helped the Electoral Tribunal to clarify and standardize its criteria for how to better provide services to citizens, improved its ability to identify the beginning and end of each of its services, set aside the concept of departments, and focused on the interaction of activities and processes. In this sense, the electoral body has changed the way in which it provides services to the population, going from routine activities to documented processes controlled by internal audits that enhance and strengthen systems.

Among the project's beneficiaries are Panama's citizens, since some of the services provided by the departments subject to certification have a direct impact on the population. These services include the production of identity cards and other documents by the civil registry, which has a direct impact on all Panamanian citizens throughout their lives.

Figure 6.3 ISO-certified processes in Panama

Responsible office	Core certified processes
Department of the Civil Registry	1. Vital records (Birth certificates) 2. Judicial processes 3. Vital records (Death certificates)
Department of Identification	1. ID card processing procedures 2. ID card supplies acquisitions 3. ID card issuing 4. ID card delivery
Department of Electoral Organization	1. Control of voter registry 2. Voter registration updating 3. Voter registration updating 4. Electoral map elaboration and distribution
Information Technology Department	1. Design and management of information technology support

Source: Department of Electoral Cooperation and Observation, Organization of American States.

The Peruvian certification

In 2010, the JNE, the Peruvian electoral body that exercises jurisdictional power, requested OAS support with the certification of the oversight of electoral processes, citizen services, civic education and legislation under ISO 9001:2008 (see Figure 6.4).

In addition, support processes such as logistics, human resources, statistics and technological development, as well as planning, innovation and development were certified.

A comprehensive assessment was conducted of the sub-processes, activities, documentation and current records of the key processes, including management, support and improvement processes. Through a series of interviews with staff, the gaps between the current practice of the electoral body and the requirements of ISO 9001:2008 were identified. This project was a major challenge at the beginning, due to the initial levels of process compliance with ISO 9001:2000 norms identified through the diagnostic. However, on completion of the process the results were extremely positive.

Figure 6.4 Four key certified processes in Peru

Processes	Sub-processes
Oversight of electoral processes	- Voter registry - General elections, elections to the Andean Parliament, regional elections, referendums and revocations - Internal democracy - Elections for civil society representatives to the Comites de Coordination Regional (CCR), Comites de Coordination Local Provincial (CCLP) and Comites de Coordination Local Distrital (CCLD) - Other electoral processes - Political party committees - Elections to municipal authorities
Citizen services	- Correspondence office - Voter exemption certificates - Citizen orientation - ROP registration - Central archive
Civic education	- Early citizen education - Continued citizen education - Women and citizenship - Electoral museum - Centre for electoral documentation
Registration of political organizations	- Registration of political organizations - Requests for and updates to political organization records - Revocation of registration - ROP archive
Regulations	- Report creation - Legislative systematization - Development of legal projects

Source: Department of Electoral Cooperation and Observation, Organization of American States.
Note: ROP = Registry of Political Organizations.

Based on the needs of the electoral body, 74 sessions of nine different training workshops were conducted on QMS-related topics (see Figure 6.5). A total of 1157 officials were trained on aspects such as process management, service quality and customer-oriented communication.

Figure 6.5 Courses and training sessions in Peru

Training Workshops	Programmed Events
Executive Analysis and Impact of ISO 9001:2008 Norms in an Organization	1
Fundamentals of ISO 9001:2008 and general methodology for implementation	10
Process Management	10
Process Mapping and Organization Objectives Deployment	10
Performance indicators Management (results)	10
Drafting of documentation and document control procedures and archival of Quality Management System 9001:2008	10
Quality tools and continuous improvement	10
Training of Internal Auditors to conduct quality management system ISO 9001:2008 19011:2002 audits	3
Quality services and customer oriented communication	10

Source: Department of Electoral Cooperation and Observation, Organization of American States.

As in the Panamanian case, both central and support processes were properly documented. The methodology was based on identifying macro-organizational processes, defining key performance indicators, and subsequently reducing these to small processes that form the basis for the definition of procedures and activities. A quality policy was drafted to regulate the body's processes and services (see Box 6.1).

The implementation of a QMS allowed the EMB to improve its services while at the same time identifying which of these services can be carried out by external providers in order to improve their efficiency.

Box 6.1 The JNE quality policy

Quality Policy

The National Electoral Jury aware of its responsibility as an autonomous constitutional and governing body of the Peruvian electoral system agrees to:

- Address its actions towards the defense of democratic and ethical principals within the framework of the Constitution and laws, to guarantee the compliance with the popular will.

- Contribute to the civic-electoral education and the strengthening of democracy in order to educate a population that is aware and committed to future generations.

- Contribute to strengthening of democracy through legislative initiatives on electoral matters.

- Guarantee the rights of political organizations and its citizens, to be expressions of political pluralism.

- Supervise the legality of the right to vote of its citizens.

- Resolve with fairness and transparency matters related to the law.

- Promote participation and commitment of its personnel with Vision, Mission and Strategic Institutional Objectives.

- Continuously improve personnel performance in order to achieve citizens' satisfaction.

Source: Jurado Nacional Elecciones de Perú. Translated from Spanish by the Department of Electoral Cooperation and Observation, Organization of American States. The original text is available at <http://portal.jne.gob.pe/Archivos/Gesti%C3%B3n%20de%20Calidad/politica_calidad.pdf>.

The Costa Rican certification

In 2008, the OAS assisted the Electoral Tribunal of Costa Rica in carrying out a diagnostic for the documentation, implementation and certification of two of its key processes: the civil registry and the electoral process. Each process was broken down into a series of sub-processes that were included in the diagnosis (see Figure 6.6).

The project identified the requirements and actions needed to implement and achieve the standardization of the EMB's processes in accordance with ISO standards. The diagnosis delivered a strategic plan, a feasibility study, a gap analysis and detailed work plan, an organizational structure analysis and the mapping of all key and support processes.

An analysis of the strengths, weaknesses, opportunities and threats (SWOT) of the electoral body was also conducted. This analysis identified positive factors such as the credibility of the electoral body, the forward-looking vision of its magistrates and the institution's citizen-focused approach as the key foundations for the implementation of a QMS within the institution. The diagnostic provided the Electoral Tribunal of Costa Rica with an important tool that will help it make the changes needed to implement a QMS.

Figure 6.6 Objectives and scope of the diagnostic in Costa Rica

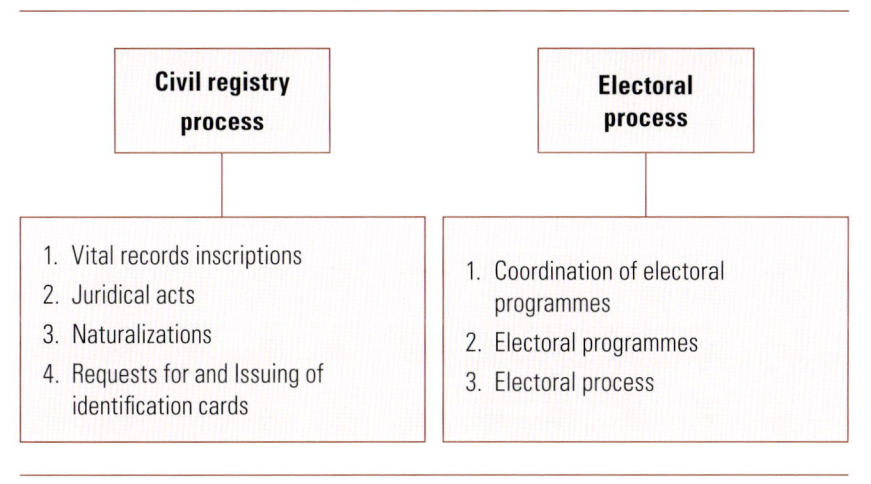

Civil registry process
1. Vital records inscriptions
2. Juridical acts
3. Naturalizations
4. Requests for and Issuing of identification cards

Electoral process
1. Coordination of electoral programmes
2. Electoral programmes
3. Electoral process

Source: Department of Electoral Cooperation and Observation, Organization of American States.

The adoption of an international electoral ISO standard

Every electoral system has its own set of regulations that vary between countries and, especially in federal systems, between regions. However, all electoral systems are composed of a series of interrelated processes conducted by three main actors: EMBs, political parties and citizens.

The benefits achieved through the implementation of a QMS by electoral bodies have raised the need to standardize the processes to be certified by ISO standards. In response to the interest expressed by some OAS member states, an ISO standard exclusively for the electoral sector is now being developed.

As is noted above, EMBs are responsible for facilitating and ensuring the transfer of power through the organization of inclusive, clean, competitive and periodic elections. The creation of the electoral ISO is designed to facilitate oversight of these and ensuring the quality of electoral processes, providing high standards of organization, efficiency and management while simultaneously encouraging the further development of democracy and respect for the will of the voters.

It is not the intention of this international standard to imply uniformity in the structure of EMBs or electoral documentation. The requirements of the electoral QMS are complementary to the product and service requirements of the EMB.

As an essential part of the development of the norm, the OAS formed a working group, putting representatives from the region's EMBs in charge of elaborating the new standard. This working group concluded that the essential elements of the organization of an election are:

1) voter registration;
2) registration of political organizations and candidates;
3) electoral logistics and planning;
4) vote casting;
5) vote counting and the declaration of results;
6) civic electoral education; and
7) oversight of campaign financing.

The working group is currently working to establish the minimum requirements for an EMB's implementation of these electoral processes. All the requirements of the electoral standard are generic and intended to be applicable to all EMBs involved in any aspect of the electoral process, regardless of whether they are permanent or temporary organizations established in support of a particular election period. The international standard is applicable to elections for all levels of government, including local, regional and national processes.

Among other things, the electoral standard should safeguard key electoral processes from the point of view of the generation of the results expected by citizens of their electoral bodies; and provide a flexible structure that permits the continual improvement of electoral bodies in order to respond adequately to the diverse challenges presented by elections. In this sense, we should not forget that the goal of elections is related not only to the legality of their results, but also to legitimacy which translates into social acceptance of the results. Therefore, the relationships between management and product quality provide critical data that give greater certainty to the various actors involved.

Finally, it is expected that this international standard could also be used by internal or external parties, including certification bodies, to assess an EMB's ability to meet citizens', statutory and regulatory requirements for electoral processes and services, along with the requirements of the EMB itself.

Conclusions

In the past, QMS and certification under ISO standards were quite foreign to the public sector, but they have become a new challenge for the institutional strengthening of EMBs, which gives them the ability to innovate and to reinvent themselves.

An institution modernizes its processes when the concept of quality is inherent in the provision of its goods and services, where the focus is the citizen's satisfaction, and where improvisation is minimal and management professional. As the concept of quality management is introduced throughout an entire EMB, it will doubtless have a positive effect on the organization of elections.

In this sense, in a context where democratic systems are facing new threats to the legitimacy of electoral processes, quality management and certification under ISO quality standards are innovative and technically feasible ways to face these challenges effectively.

Quality management as a tool for improving performance will result in more transparent and efficient EMBs with processes that are better aligned with their objectives. Through the implementation of a QMS, the EMB demonstrates its openness and transparency to society and its willingness to be periodically evaluated by external auditors using international standards.

The EMBs that have already started on the road to quality should remember that taking that first step will lead them to new and more efficient ways of carrying out their responsibilities, and that the importance of this change will provide the consistency and discipline that will make such a change sustainable.

The OAS is interested in promoting this important tool and hopes that additional EMBs will adopt quality management in their institutions as a permanent practice. This will undoubtedly result in a reform or reinvention of relations between states and their citizens, helping to increase the integrity of the EMB at all levels, from improving its ability to provide services to citizens, to increasing the confidence of citizens in their institutions, and by creating increased capacity for the organization to conduct fair and transparent electoral processes.

References and further reading

Diaz, Cristian Venegas and Herrera, Heidi Berner, 'Chile: External ISO Standards Certificate of Management Improvement Programs in the Public Sector', chapter in *Emerging Good Practices in Managing for Development Results*, 2nd edn (Naperville, IL: Sourcebooks, 2007)

International Organization for Standardization, 'Quality Management Principles', available at <http://www.iso.org/iso/qmp>

Lowery, Daniel, ISO 9000: 'A Certification-Based Technology Reinventing the Federal Government', *Public Productivity and Management Review*, 22/2 (December 2008), pp. 232–50

Martinez, Magdiel, 'Panama's Electoral Tribunal Quality Management System: Third Party Audit Experience', *Revista Mundo Electoral*, 4/10 (January 2010)

Milakovic, Michael E., *Total Quality Management for Public Sector Productivity Improvement* (Armonk, NY: M. E. Sharpe, Inc., 1990)

OAS, 'La experiencia panameña de gestión de calidad en el área electoral', by Pablo Gutiérrez, *Revista Mundo Electoral*, 2009

Proyecto Bid 02/10, 'Implementación del Sistema de Gestión de la Calidad (ISO 9001:2008) en el Jurado Nacional de Elecciones (JNE) de la República del Perú', 2010

Stirton, Lindsay and Lodge, Martin, 'Transparency Mechanisms: Building Publicness into Public Services' (Oxford: Blackwell Publishing on behalf of Cardiff University, 2001)

United Nations Economic and Social Commission for Asia, 'Application of ISO 9000 Standards in Local Government and Other Public Sector Organizations', New York, 2001

Notes

[1] For more information see the website of the International Organization for Standardization (ISO) at <http://www.iso.org>.
[2] Since it was first published over 20 years ago, ISO 9001 has become the most successful QMS standard in the world.
[3] Quality Management Principles, ISO website, available at <http://www.iso.org>.

Chapter 7

Election Observation by
the Pacific Islands Forum:
Experiences and Challenges

Chapter 7

Henry Ivarature

Election Observation by the Pacific Islands Forum: Experiences and Challenges[1]

Introduction

In 2011, the Pacific Islands Forum (PIF) celebrated ten years of its election observation programme (EOP) and its special relationship with the Biketawa Declaration. The EOP is an integral part of the maturity of the Biketawa Declaration, which profiles the PIF's role in monitoring electoral systems that are crucial to promoting representative democracy and protecting the integrity of democratic institutions in the Pacific Islands. This coincided with the 40th anniversary of the PIF's existence as a regional organization.

Since the PIF observed the general elections in the Solomon Islands in 2001, 17 election observation missions (EOMs) have been deployed. The Forum Observer Group (FOG) has observed general elections in nine of the 16 Forum island countries (FICs), including the Autonomous Region of Bougainville. Altogether, 48 observers, excluding PIF Secretariat and Commonwealth Secretariat officials, have participated in the EOMs. Collectively, they have made a total of 142 recommendations, all of which aimed to strengthen the election process, improve electoral management practices and enhance electoral laws and regulations. All these recommendations have been made in support of good governance and the rule of law, and in the spirit of protecting the integrity of the electoral system.

This chapter uses three case studies to share the election observation experiences of the PIF. The case studies were selected because they account for nine of the 17 EOMs deployed by the PIF. In describing EOM practice in the Solomon Islands, the Autonomous Region of Bougainville and Nauru, the chapter discusses observation processes and challenges, makes some suggestions to improve observation practice and explores a framework for following up on EOM recommendations.

The Pacific Islands Forum and its Secretariat

The PIF has a membership of 16 sovereign independent states in the Pacific Islands region. As the key intergovernmental organization, it plays a leading role in promoting the region's political and economic agendas. Its members are the four Melanesian states of Fiji, Papua New Guinea (PNG), the Solomon Islands and Vanuatu, the Micronesian states of the Federated States of Micronesia (FSM), Nauru, Palau, Kiribati and the Republic of the Marshall Islands (RMI), and the Polynesian states of the Cook Islands, Niue, Samoa, Tonga and Tuvalu, as well as Australia and New Zealand. It is the only regional organization with such political standing in the Pacific region.

The PIF is the initiative of the region's visionary leaders, who recognized its political value as a regional body in which Pacific Island leaders could discuss common issues and the shared challenges related to politics, trade and services. The PIF also discusses common approaches to find regional solutions to such challenges. It serves as the regional voice of the Pacific Islands, collectively articulating its position on regional, international and global issues. Developing from an informal gathering of leaders, the PIF has matured to take on a formal and defined structure. In 2005, leaders adopted a new agreement establishing the PIF as an intergovernmental organization under international law (Spillane 2008). The agreement updates the purpose and function of the PIF to reflect its vision and direction under the Pacific Plan. In order to facilitate regional cooperation and integration, leaders of the PIF agreed to broaden its membership by establishing new associate and observer membership categories (Pacific Islands Forum 2009). Tokelau, Wallis and Futuna, the Commonwealth and the Asian Development Bank are observers at the PIF and Timor Leste is a special observer.

The agenda of the PIF is based on reports from the PIF Secretariat and the related regional organizations and committees, ministerial meetings and members. Forum leaders' decisions are arrived at through consensus and are outlined in a Forum Communiqué, from which regional programmes are developed and implemented. The head of government of the country that hosts the annual PIF meeting is the chair of the PIF until the next meeting. The PIF is the only intergovernmental body in the region whose gatherings are attended by the democratically elected political leaders of independent and self-governing states. The nature of its membership and the directions it sets on major issues for the region mean that the positions the PIF takes have political weight, authority and legitimacy. The decisions of the PIF are acted on by a number of players, including the donor community and development partners. The priorities it sets for the region are used as a point of reference by regional and international organizations, and its decisions act as subtle political direction for its members and the international community.

The administrative arm of the PIF is the PIF Secretariat, which is based in Suva. It serves as the Secretariat for PIF-related events, implements the decisions of PIF leaders, facilitates the delivery of development assistance to member state governments, and undertakes the political and legal mandates of PIF meetings. The Secretariat is headed by a Secretary General. The current incumbent is Tuiloma Neroni Slade of Samoa. The governing body of the PIF Secretariat is the PIF Officials Committee, made up of representatives of all member state governments. The Secretary General is also the permanent Chair of the Council of Regional Organizations in the Pacific, which has a membership of 11 regional organizations such as the PIF Fisheries Agency, the South Pacific Environmental Programme and the Secretariat of the Pacific Community. The Pacific Plan Action Committee, which is made up of officials from all the FICs, is also chaired by the Secretary General who oversees the implementation of the Pacific Plan. The Pacific Plan, which the PIF endorsed in 2005, identifies a number of regional priorities under four pillars: economic growth, sustainable development, good governance and security, which are all geared to achieving greater regional integration and cooperation.

A mandate to observe elections

The Biketawa Declaration and the three key principles

The mandate for the PIF to deploy EOMs and to observe general elections in the FICs is derived from the Biketawa Declaration which was endorsed by leaders in 2000. It is something like the political manifesto of the PIF on democracy, democratic values, the liberties of citizens, equal rights of citizens, the rule of law and democratic political processes. The guiding principles in the Biketawa Declaration mandate the PIF, at the request of its member states, to assist, through a process of consultation, when these core values might be significantly affected by a situation of national conflict or crisis.

However, the sovereignty of the PIF member states is of paramount importance and the Biketawa Declaration unequivocally supports the principle of non-interference in the domestic affairs of its member states. EOMs cannot be commissioned unless the PIF is invited in by an FIC. The three primary principles in the Biketawa Declaration that mandate the PIF to deploy EOMs in FICs are:

1) commitment to good governance, which is the exercise of authority (leadership) and interactions in a manner that is open, transparent, accountable, participatory, consultative and decisive but fair and equitable;
2) belief in the liberty of the individual under the law, in equal rights for all citizens regardless of gender, race, colour, creed or political belief, and in the individual's inalienable right to participate by means of a free and democratic political process in framing the society in which he or she lives; and
3) upholding democratic processes and institutions which reflect national and local circumstances, including the transfer of power, the rule of law and the independence of the judiciary, and just and honest government (Pacific Islands Forum 2000).

Essentially, the PIF will deploy EOMs at the invitation or request of a member state government. Consistent with the three principles of the Biketawa Declaration, the EOM will observe that citizens' rights to participate freely and fairly in the election process are protected according to national law.

EOMs and the PIF Observer Group: an extension of the 'Secretary General's good offices role'

The PIF has deployed EOMs to Samoa (2011), Niue (2011), the Cook Island (2010), the Solomon Islands (2010, 2006 and 2001), Nauru (2010, 2008, 2007 and 2004), the Autonomous Region of Bougainville (2010 and 2005), the RMI (2008 and 2007), PNG (2007), Fiji (2006) and Vanuatu (2004). All but three of these missions were full EOMs. The EOMs to Samoa and Niue, for instance, were arranged at such extremely short notice that logistical complexities made it impossible to arrange for the full participation of PIF observers. Eight EOMs have been deployed to FICs in the Melanesian group of islands, but so far only three general elections have been observed in FICs in Polynesia. The PIF has deployed five EOMs in the Micronesian group of islands, with Nauru accounting for four of these.

EOMs and the FOGs are commissioned through the good offices of the Secretary General. Invitations from FICs to the PIF to observe general elections are usually submitted through the ministry of foreign affairs to the

Secretary General of the PIF. The PIF has received invitations from prime ministers (Solomon Islands 2005 and Fiji 2006), presidents (Nauru 2004) and foreign ministers (Nauru 2007). An unprecedented case was that of the RMI, where the Nitijela (parliament) passed a resolution calling on the executive to invite regional and international observers.

On receipt of a request, the Secretary General informs the PIF Chair of the appointment of the FOG, and furnishes other relevant information such as the period of deployment of the EOM and the FOG's terms of reference. Thereafter, the Secretary General advises all member state governments of the arrangements for the deployment of the FOG and the names of the observers, including the names of the Secretariat staff assigned to support the observers. The observers are usually experts and public figures from the region appointed by the Secretary General to represent the PIF. These individuals have been authorized to observe, comment on and, where appropriate, make recommendations on a member state government's management of its elections, and identify areas that may strengthen electoral laws, practices and procedures. This is set out in the terms of reference agreed by the FICs before the FOG is deployed.

When observers are appointed by the Secretary General they participate in their own right, as representatives of the PIF, and not as representatives of governments. Observers report their findings in a written report that is submitted to the Secretary General. Sometimes, the Chair of the FOG may also meet with the Secretary General to personally hand over the report and discuss key elements. Because it is appointed by and reports directly to the Secretary General, the FOG is an extension of the role of 'Secretary General's good offices'. Electoral experts, including election managers, form the core body of the observers relied on by the PIF in all EOMs. The head of large EOMs is usually an eminent person such as a former or current parliamentarian, a former head of government, a constitutional office-holder or, as was the case for Fiji's general elections in 2006, the Secretary General of the PIF. Pacific Islanders of high standing, including a Speaker of a parliament, electoral experts, senior election managers, senior government officials and academics, have accepted invitations from the Secretary General to observe elections on behalf of the PIF.

Before observing the conduct of polling, the FOG, as is common practice for all EOMs, calls on the country's Minister for Foreign Affairs, the electoral management body (EMB) and the heads of the country's law enforcement agencies, as well as consulting other stakeholders such as candidates in the election, leaders of political parties, leaders of the opposition, government ministers, members of the business community, members of the media, leaders of the main churches, leaders of non-governmental organizations (NGOs), foreign diplomats, and men and women of high standing in their communities. The period of a general election is a busy one for many stakeholders and securing meetings can be a challenge. The primary purpose is to gather as much information as possible on the preparations for the elections by the government and the EMB, and areas of the electoral system that may need to be strengthened—and to gain a general appreciation of the political climate and the environment in which the general election is being held.

The FOG's report is presented to the Secretary General immediately after the election. The report is signed by the Chair of the FOG and the observers, or the head of the EOM. Similarly, the letter conveying the report is signed either by the Chair of the FOG or by all the observers or the head of the EOM. The FOG report is presented by the Secretary General to the Prime Minister or the President of the FIC in which the election was observed. Copies of the FOG report are also presented to the Minister of Foreign Affairs, the head of the EMB, leaders of the opposition and leaders of the major political parties. The Secretary General also informs the government that on receipt of the report it will be circulated to all the FICs, placed on the website of the PIF Secretariat and subsequently publicized.

Two recent EOMs (Samoa in 2011 and Niue in 2011) were undertaken by officials of the PIF Secretariat. No observers were appointed to these EOMs because, as is noted above, the request was made at very short notice. Nonetheless, reports were submitted to the Secretary General and conveyed to the respective governments for their comments. However, some policy guidelines are required to govern this practice in future. A policy-defining question would be whether the PIF Secretariat should deploy EOMs without the appointment of an observer or observers, even if the EOM is requested by an FIC. Alternatively, such missions could continue to be treated as part of the Secretariat's work programme.

Domestic guidelines for international election observers

The PIF was invited to observe the general election in the Solomon Islands in 2001. The government developed basic guidelines for election observers, International and Local Observers: Terms of Reference and Code of Conduct, to be issued to all the observer groups that came to the Solomon Islands. At that time, the PIF only had the general guidelines contained in the Biketawa

Declaration. The PIF continued to use these general guidelines until it endorsed the Declaration of Principles for International Election Observation and the Code of Conduct for International Election Observers in 2005, which now serve as the PIF's guidelines for EOMs. For the 2006 general election in the Solomon Islands, the Solomon Islands Electoral Commission prepared new guidelines for observers, the Code of Conduct: Ethical and Professional Observations of Elections, which it again issued to all observers. Only the Solomon Islands, Fiji and PNG, including the Autonomous Region of Bougainville, had developed domestic guidelines for observers as of 2010.[2]

As EOMs become standard practice for FICs, it would be useful for the PIF to initiate a regional meeting of EMBs, observers appointed by the PIF and other international observers and electoral experts to promote EOMs and help FICs understand the importance of EOMs, the obligations on FICs set out in the Declaration of Principles and the Code of Conduct, and how these could be better articulated in domestic guidelines for international election observers. Moreover, as concern grows that the national elections of the FICs should be open and transparent, including through the monitoring exercises of EOMs, it is imperative that the FICs that lack domestic guidelines for international observers should develop these in consultation with other EMBs, observers and electoral experts. These are areas that others involved in election observation in the region could consider supporting.

The electoral laws of the FICs do not contain specific provisions on domestic or international observers or EOMs. Moreover, these electoral laws often do not allow observers to monitor all aspects of the electoral process. In some FICs, such as the Cook Islands, Nauru and Niue, observers are not permitted to be inside the polling station or to observe counting. Usually, election managers and chief electoral officers use their discretionary powers to permit observers to see the polling and the counting of votes. Some electoral laws have provisions on discretionary powers which are invoked by EMBs to permit accredited observers to monitor election processes. Obviously, these are areas that need to be examined in consultation with EMBs, governments and electoral experts, including the election observer community. Appropriate provisions governing domestic and international observers could be integrated into electoral systems in order to cater for EOMs.

The PIF's endorsement of the Declaration of Principles and Code of Conduct

In 2005, the need was already evident inside the PIF Secretariat for the PIF to develop its own internal set of guidelines for EOMs. It was therefore a timely coincidence that the PIF was approached by the three main initiators of the final draft of Declaration of Principles and the Code of Conduct to review the document and to consider endorsing it at the United Nations. The initiators were the National Democratic Institute (NDI), the United Nations Electoral Assistance Division (UNEAD) and the Carter Center.

The PIF, through the offices of the Secretary General, readily supported the Declaration of Principles in October 2005, along with 23 other regional and international organizations. The Declaration of Principles and the Code of Conduct elaborate on the three guiding principles of the Biketawa Declaration and on the PIF's support to democracy, democratic institutions and the rights of citizens to participate in the governance of their societies through free, fair and democratic elections held according to national law. More work is needed, however, on developing and strengthening national guidelines to complement the universal guidelines.

It is therefore important for the PIF Secretariat, through a meeting of EMBs, to share the Declaration of Principles and the Code of Conduct with all the FICs so that their EMBs understand and appreciate their obligations. This may improve some FICs' perception of EOMs and could ideally lead to the development of a regional election observation framework for members of the PIF. Although the PIF endorsed the Declaration of Principles and the Code of Conduct, the universal guidelines remain to be shared with the FICs.

Joint EOMs: the PIF and the Commonwealth

Thus far, the PIF has undertaken joint EOMs with only one organization: the Commonwealth. Eleven FICs are also members of the Commonwealth (Australia, the Cook Islands, Kiribati, Nauru, New Zealand, PNG, Samoa, the Solomon Islands, Tonga, Tuvalu and Vanuatu). In addition to this degree of commonality, both organizations have committed themselves in a memorandum of understanding to collaborate on a range of activities. The Commonwealth–PIF partnership began in 2001 when both organizations collaborated to deploy a joint EOM to observe the general election in the Solomon Islands. As is noted above, this joint EOM was also the inaugural EOM of the PIF.

The PIF and the Commonwealth deployed joint EOMs to Nauru and Vanuatu in 2004, the Autonomous Region of Bougainville in 2005 and Papua New Guinea in 2007. This partnership accounts for five of the EOMs undertaken by the PIF. In fact, the first four EOMs of the PIF were jointly undertaken with the Commonwealth. The majority of the observers who have participated in joint EOMs are from the Pacific region. Altogether, 14 observers have been engaged, supported by 18 officers from the PIF Secretariat and the Commonwealth Secretariat. The joint EOMs made a total of 39 recommendations. Observer reports prepared by a joint EOM are presented by the leader of the observers to the two Secretaries General. The heads of the Commonwealth and the PIF then jointly present the report to the Prime Minister or the President of the FIC government whose general election was observed. This practice has been consistently applied in all five of the joint EOMs.

These joint EOMs have been useful for the PIF in developing its EOP. They also laid a sound platform for the PIF to undertake joint EOMs with other organizations. Electoral experts from the FICs have also participated in Commonwealth EOMs elsewhere. At least two Pacific Island electoral experts engaged by the PIF have also been appointed as observers by the Commonwealth. While the number remains small, this nevertheless provides opportunities for Pacific Island electoral experts to gain knowledge of election systems outside the region. It also helps observers to draw on these experiences in order to further strengthen the electoral systems in their own countries.

Strengths and weaknesses

Case study 1: The Solomon Islands

As is noted above, the PIF deployed EOMs to the Solomon Islands in 2001, 2006 and 2010. Each was undertaken in different political circumstances. The 2001 EOM was undertaken when the Solomon Islands, some 20 years after attaining its independence from the United Kingdom, was besieged by lawlessness, ethnic conflict and tension. By 2000, the law and order situation had deteriorated to such an extent that businesses were forced to close, government services were no longer functioning and the police force was ineffective. The Prime Minister, Bartholomew Ulufa'alu, was taken hostage and forced to resign on 14 June 2000, to be replaced by Manasseh Sogovare. Peace was brokered between the conflicting parties on 15 October 2000, resulting in the Townsville Peace Accord which paved the way for a long process of restoring public order, rebuilding public services and supporting the return of trade and commerce. The 2001 general election was of such significance that it attracted more than 80 international observers from international, regional and development agencies.

This high level of representation, and the high-level consultations between the Chair of the PIF and the Secretary General, aside from ensuring the integrity of the election process, clearly demonstrate the importance the PIF attached to this EOM. Three eminent Pacific Islanders were appointed as observers: an Ombudsman and former Secretary to the Government and

Samoa's first Ambassador to the United Nations, who chaired the FOG; a Director of a health service and former Vice-President of the Federated States of Micronesia; and a learned woman member of the PNG judiciary. Their report, however, has not been made public.

The 2006 EOM was deployed after the political situation had improved following the intervention of the Regional Assistance Mission to the Solomon Islands (RAMSI). This Mission was endorsed by the PIF under the terms of the Biketawa Declaration. Ethnic conflict had continued until 2003, so it was important that the PIF and other international observers, including the United Nations Election Observation Coordination Team, observe a process that was fundamental to democracy, human rights and good governance.

Once again, the PIF deployed a high-level FOG, this time chaired by a former President of Kiribati, who was accompanied by seven observers and supported by two officials from the PIF Secretariat. The observers included the PNG Registrar of Political Parties, a Deputy Clerk of the Legislative Assembly of Samoa and four election experts. All but one were Pacific Islanders. A total of 44 international observers from Australia, Japan, New Zealand, the United States and the Commonwealth were present in the Solomon Islands. Around 80 domestic observers also took part, assisted by the Commonwealth. All these observers expressed concerns about the accuracy of and access to the register of voters, including the absence of voters' names. The FOG report was circulated to PIF member state governments on 19 April 2006. On 18 and 19 April 2006, one day before the report was circulated, violence and looting erupted in Honiara, preventing the swearing-in of Prime Minister Snyder Rini. Gangs of looters raided businesses belonging to Chinese traders and burned most of the buildings to the ground.

The 2010 EOM to the Solomon Islands was led by the PIF representative from the Solomon Islands. He was accompanied by the Acting Electoral Commissioner of the government of the Autonomous Region of Bougainville. Secretariat support was provided by three officials from the PIF Secretariat—one advisor and two officers. A total of 62 international election observers from Australia, Japan, New Zealand, South Korea, the Commonwealth and the East-West Centre also monitored the elections.

All the EOMs were undertaken as an extension of the Secretary General's good offices, with the objective of monitoring political developments and assisting with peace building in the FICs. The attention paid to the Solomon Islands in all three general elections, by a record number of international observers from different countries and organizations, provided the government and the EMB with 22 recommendations on strengthening the electoral process in the Solomon Islands. A gathering of these observers and the EMB in the Solomon Islands should ideally take place before the next general election to assess whether these recommendations were feasible and have been implemented. Since the PIF has observed all three general elections, it might be appropriate to consider a stocktaking exercise on the take-up of its recommendations.

Case study 2: The Autonomous Region of Bougainville

The PIF deployed an EOM to the Autonomous Region of Bougainville in 2005 and 2010. The 2005 general election was the first in the Autonomous Region, and the first election of a President. The island and its people had undergone a prolonged period of violence and internal conflict, which made the general election a significant political achievement for its people as well as a political symbol of self-determination.

Both the government of Papua New Guinea and Bougainville's leaders played an important role in the long and sustained period of negotiations on the political process, and in concluding the Bougainville Peace Agreement which was signed on 31 August 2001. The Agreement led to the development of a constitution for the Autonomous Region of Bougainville, which is an integral component of arrangements for political autonomy. The constitution was approved by the PNG government in 2004, which paved the way for the general election. The constitution established a legislature with its own governance and administrative structures, as well as an EMB. Such was the importance of the 2005 general election that a statement was issued by the President of the United Nations Security Council (United Nations Security Council 2005).

The 2005 EOM was a high-level delegation chaired by Ratu Epeli Nailatikau, the then Speaker of the Fiji House of Representatives. He was accompanied by five observers who were supported by three officials. It was a joint EOM with the Commonwealth, working with other international observers as an international observer team. Observers came from Australia, Fiji, Japan, Trinidad and Tobago, and Vanuatu. Logistics for the observers were coordinated by the United Nations.

The second EOM to Bougainville was considerably smaller. It was led by the Principal Electoral Officer of Vanuatu, who had also taken part in the 2005 EOM. Other international observers included representatives from Australia, the Commonwealth, the East-West Centre based in Hawai'i and the United Nations.

In both cases, invitations to observe the election were issued through the government of Papua New Guinea in consultation with the government of the Autonomous Region of Bougainville. In this case, of a newly established autonomous region, EOMs are about ensuring that the political process of electing political leaders is not only strengthened, but also entrenched over time as an integral democratic institution. This is the most fundamental aspect of the election process which the three principles of the Biketawa Declaration seek to safeguard. The fact that the Autonomous Region of Bougainville experienced a long period of conflict, and, consequently, an absence of governance structures and democratic institutions, means that EOMs will continue to play a strong role in reinforcing and consolidating democracy, the rule of law and good governance.

Case study 3: The Republic of Nauru

As is noted above, Nauru has had the benefit of four EOMs deployed by the PIF (in 2004, 2007, 2008 and 2010). The 2004 joint PIF and Commonwealth EOM to Nauru took place after the country's parliament had been dissolved, following the declaration of a state of emergency by the country's President on 30 September 2004. The decision was precipitated by strong political differences between the government and the Speaker of the parliament, which seriously affected the proper functioning of government. At the same time, after years of financial mismanagement, economic conditions had deteriorated to such an extent that government revenues were affected. Drastic measures were instituted, such as wage cuts for public servants of 80 per cent, in order to fund basic public services. The economic situation eventually led to the intervention of the PIF at the request of the government of Nauru, invoking the Biketawa Declaration. Pacific Regional Assistance to Nauru was subsequently put in place to help reform the economy. The dire political and economic conditions presented a strong rationale for an independent validation of the 2004 snap election. The President of Nauru asked the PIF to send an EOM, in line with the Biketawa Declaration.

At Nauru's invitation, the PIF observed the 2007 general election and the second snap election eight months later. Essentially, the 2008 EOM was an extension of the 2007 EOM. Political differences and instability after the 2007 general election forced President Marcus Stephen to dissolve parliament and call a fresh election. Perhaps in response to the political circumstances in 2008, the EOM's terms of reference included the unprecedented task of monitoring the parliamentary and political consequences of the election, and making any additional recommendations which might be appropriate (Pacific Islands Forum 2008a). Only three recommendations were made, which supported the national agenda for constitutional reforms to strengthen political stability, accountability and the clarity of governance institutions (Pacific Islands Forum 2008a).

The 2010 general election was held one year ahead of schedule, based on a normal three-year parliamentary term. The President of Nauru advised the Speaker to dissolve parliament after opposition members attempted to oust the government in a series of no-confidence motions. The incumbents were re-elected but, after several attempts to elect a Speaker failed, the people of Nauru went to the polls again within a few weeks. All the members of parliament (MPs) except one were re-elected, but a government could not be formed for several months. A parliament of 18 members and the inability of one political group to dominate mean that it is not unusual for a 'hung parliament' to emerge.

Nauru accounts for 30 of the 142 recommendations made by PIF observers. While recognizing the sovereignty of FICs, arrangements should be made to follow up these recommendations. However, Nauru's real challenge is more of a political nature than an electoral one. It is about strengthening parliament and other governance institutions and addressing political instability. All the PIF EOMs concluded that the elections in Nauru were credible and reflected the will of the people. Without action on these recommendations, future EOMs may end up just restating them. Snap elections cannot be ruled out unless political leaders confront the real political issues and introduce appropriate political and governance reforms that nurture and sustain political stability and good governance.

Prospects and recommendations

From the short-term to the long-term

After ten years of EOM experience uninterrupted by an internal review, it may be time for the PIF to evaluate its EOP. Ideally, such a review would help set out the future and short-term directions of the EOP, and how the PIF Secretariat proposes to implement them. On average, the PIF has deployed two EOMs per year. However, since 2007 the average number of EOMs deployed has increased to three, and four EOMs were deployed in 2010. If this trend is a positive indication of interest in EOMs by FICs, the PIF Secretariat may need to review how it manages the EOP in order to meet the potential demand.

Other issues in the short term include developing an internal operations manual governing the procedures for the appointment of observers, the appointment of Secretariat officials, and the protocols and procedures for strengthening the Secretary General's good offices role on the commissioning of EOMs. Other important questions include improving communication between FICs and the Office of the Secretary General as well as the Chair of the PIF, the communication of the reports from observers to the Secretary General and to FICs, and the disclosure of EOM reports.

Other aspects include the harmonization and standardization of EOM reports, clearly defining what constitutes a proper EOM as opposed to a PIF Secretariat mission, and how the reports from the latter's exercises are governed with respect to the country observed and disclosure. Further consideration should also be given to developing a register of observers, which has been attempted in the past, to enable the PIF to draw on a wider pool of election managers in the region. One important attribute of EOMs is their capacity to help election managers see how elections are managed elsewhere and use this experience to strengthen their own electoral systems. So far, the PIF has utilized the expertise of electoral officials from seven FICs. Six of these electoral experts have participated in more than two EOMs. One has been engaged in five EOMs. A regional balance and fair representation may be a consideration for the EOP.

Long-term considerations depend on the amount of budgetary support the PIF Secretariat is prepared to invest in the EOP. This may be subject to three policy considerations. The first is whether the EOP should observe the general elections held in all the FICs, or whether it should be more selective. In the latter case, the PIF could confine its observation programme to general elections in which democracy and democratic institutions, the rule of law and the rights of citizens to free and fair elections have a tendency to be affected by the residual effects of internal social or ethnic conflict or the spin-offs from political instability. The second policy consideration is whether EOPs should maintain the status quo, that is, wait to be asked in by FICs and then proceed to deploy EOMs accordingly, subject to other commitments, the availability of advisors and budgetary constraints.

The final policy consideration, which is a cross-cutting issue, is whether the EOP would consider following up the recommendations of the EOMs. This would add another dimension to both the above policy considerations, and confronts the difficult dimension of politics and its associated sensitivities. These three policy considerations have the potential to determine the scale and scope of the PIF's EOP.

Follow-up

The subject of follow-up can be classified into three broad areas. The first is about ascertaining whether the recommendations made by EOMs are practical and feasible, have been considered and have been implemented by EMBs. This is an area which remains to be progressed. The total number of recommendations from all the PIF EOM reports so far is 142. Nauru, which has invited in four EOMS, has 30 recommendations, the Solomon Islands 22 and the Autonomous Region of Bougainville 11. The PIF has not audited these recommendations and a review is perhaps necessary not only because it would show whether FICs have done something about improving the quality of their election management processes and electoral systems, but also to avoid potential wastage of resources in deploying EOMs if nothing is done about the recommendations and these same recommendations are re-articulated.

The second aspect of follow-up is a possible extension of the EOMs, that is, to monitor post-election developments. Undertaking this exercise would be expensive but it would represent complete coverage of the entire election process. An important aspect of the observation process is monitoring disputed elections and by-elections. Terms of reference requiring observers to be present in the FIC holding general elections 'before, during and after' elections would technically extend the period of observations. This includes monitoring the outcomes of the dispute and if necessary observing by-elections.

The third aspect of follow-up is to address issues which are not confined to general elections. Without necessarily devaluing the importance of an election and its relevance to promoting participatory democracy, the real challenges in many FICs whose elections have been observed are political and developmental in nature rather than strictly about elections. General elections do not occur in a vacuum: they are played out as an integral part of a multi-faceted socio-political and socio-economic process. Holistic approaches aimed at addressing genuine political and development issues would in the long term help to produce a conducive environment for free and fair elections. Following up on the recommendations of EOMs, on monitoring post-election developments and on the broader challenges of politics are important considerations for the future.

Development of regional norms

At least three regional norms are evident from the actual practice of EOMs. The first is the underlying consideration for the sovereignty and independence of FICs, which the Biketawa Declaration recognizes through its policy of non-interference in the domestic affairs of FICs. As FICs gradually open up their electoral systems and the management of elections to external scrutiny, the interface between the principle of non-interference in domestic affairs and the demand for transparency, accountability and good governance becomes increasingly well-defined. This could mean that scrutiny should be welcomed but decisions on the take-up of recommendations left to each FIC. An important point here is that the PIF and other organizations interested in observing an FIC's general election ought not to proceed until an invitation has been issued. This regional norm is articulated in the Declaration of Principles and the Code of Conduct, and expressed in the Biketawa Declaration. It is a regional norm that is strictly adhered to by the PIF.

The second regional norm is an extension of the first. A general understanding prevails in the region on the appointment of prominent and eminent Pacific Islanders as chairpersons of the FOGs, and the appointment of Pacific Island electoral experts, mixed with a few external observers, to the EOMs. The sensitivities that FICs have about their electoral systems make the appointment of eminent Pacific Islanders as representatives of the PIF through the good offices role of the Secretary General an invaluable practice. It has not only reduced the potential tension between non-interference and being invited in, but also helped significantly to promote good governance in elections. One factor that supports this development is observers making recommendations within the confines of their terms of reference, focusing primarily on elections.

The general tendency in the region is for EOMs to be focused on FICs with some history of political instability, a reputation of sorts for troublesome and problematic electioneering and a history of democratic elections being occasionally disrupted due to an unconstitutional assumption of political power or a prolonged period of conflict and violence. Evidence from the PIF EOMs confirms this somewhat inadvertent bias in EOMs deployed by the PIF. Nonetheless, these EOMs are consistent with the collective interests of the PIF and the spirit of the Biketawa Declaration, that is, to promote good governance and the rule of law, and to see that democratic processes are upheld.

Alternatives to election observation: meetings of EMBs

EMBs should be encouraged to gather to discuss their electoral laws and procedures for election management and voter registration, polling, and the counting and declaration of results. EOMs have scrutinized the management and conduct of elections by EMBs. However, the transfer of knowledge, including recommendations, is largely one-way. Interactions and exchanges between EMBs and EOMs should be organized in the region, building on and linking up with electoral strengthening projects.

EOMs are invaluable as an independent analysis of the conduct and integrity of FICs' election processes. They also ensure the confidence of voters and governments. The recommendations of EOMs are essentially the informed advice of electoral experts at a particular period of time on how the electoral process might be improved. EOMs should therefore continue, but a regular gathering of EMBs could complement the work of EOMs. The PIF could use such a gathering to present and promote the Declaration of Principles and the Code of Conduct to all its members. FICs with experience of elections being observed by EOMs could also share their own experiences of the value of EOMs in strengthening good governance. A regional gathering of EMBs has the potential to facilitate opportunities for regional cooperation, including the pooling and sharing of regional resources, expertise and technical advice in strengthening electoral systems and practices. This gathering of regional EMBs could build on the activities of the Pacific Islands, Australia and

New Zealand Administrators Network, which is a semi-formal association of electoral administrators working in the Pacific region that facilitates and encourages the free flow of electoral information among its members and, where possible, provides assistance.

Recommendations on gender in EOM reports and EOMs

As with the low number of women in Pacific legislatures, more effort is needed to improve the gender balance of EOMs. Only 11 of the 48 observers appointed between 2001 and 2011 were women (see Table 7.1). One woman observer, Makurita Baaro, a former Chief Secretary and Secretary to the Kiribati government, led two EOMs to Nauru (in 2007 and 2008). Over half the support staff assisting the observers, however, were women. Women play a key role in logistical support and drafting the election observation reports. More effort could be put into increasing the number of women observers, including those heading EOMs.

The PIF EOM reports include a section on gender issues. However, stronger consideration should be given to concrete recommendations about greater representation and political participation by women in legislatures. Such recommendations could also form part of the list of items to be followed up as part of the recommendation on follow-up. Where FICs have signed international and regional conventions such as the Convention on the Elimination of All Forms of Discrimination against Women, consideration should be given to reminding FICs of their commitments.

Conclusions: strengthening PIF election observation practice

With ten years' experience of EOMs the PIF, and the PIF Secretariat in particular, should consider a stocktake of its EOP to set its directions for the short and long term. Short-term considerations may include the development of internal guidelines to operationalize PIF-sanctioned EOMs. This is overdue and could be readily constructed based on practice and on the experiences of the deployment of EOMs. Key policy questions also need to be considered as these could potentially define the scale, scope and focus of the PIF's EOP. Key policy-defining questions include whether the EOP should be comprehensive, that is, observe all elections in FICs, or selective. Whichever option is chosen, EOMs should remain dependent on invitations from FICs.

Finally, should the PIF consider the subject of follow-up? Follow-up has important policy implications for the future direction of the EOP because it covers three fundamental processes. The first is to follow up the recommendations of the EOMs. Given the number of recommendations made so far, it is timely that these recommendations should be reviewed to see whether they were practical and feasible, and whether they have been accepted and implemented. The PIF is anxious not to be seen as interfering in the internal affairs of FICs, but should consider examining suitable frameworks for exploring this matter, including arranging meetings with EMBs.

The second type of follow-up is related to monitoring post-election political developments, including election disputes and by-elections which are an integral part of the entire election process. The final type is an acknowledgement of the fact that general elections occur in a political environment. Since political and developmental issues are the real challenges for many FICs, addressing them in the long term may allow for the development of a more enabling electoral environment that supports free and fair elections, and is consistent with human rights obligations and the rule of law.

These are serious and bold policy considerations for the PIF. They are also central to the three key principles of the Biketawa Declaration, which provides the mandate for the PIF's EOP. Addressing these policy defining questions would take the EOP to a new level, including further defining the guiding framework of the Biketawa Declaration and its relation to the FICs.

Table 7.1 Summary of EOMs and observers on Forum EOMs from 2001 to 2011

No. of EOMs	Year	FICs	Total team on EOMs	Men	Women	Total observers	No. of women as observers	No. of support officers
1	2001	Solomon Islands	6	3	3	3	1	3
2	2004	Vanuatu	4	4	0	1	0	3
3	2004	Nauru	5	5	0	2	0	3
4	2005	Bougainville	8	5	3	5	1	3
5	2006	Solomon Islands	9	5	4	7	3	2
6	2006	Fiji	21	15	6	17	3	4
7	2007	Nauru	4	1	3	2	1	2
8	2007	Papua New Guinea	8	4	4	2	0	6

9	2007	Republic of the Marshall Islands	6	3	3	3	1	3
10	2008	Republic of the Marshall Islands	1	0	1	0	0	1
11	2008	Nauru	2	2	0	1	1	1
12	2010	Bougainville	3	1	2	1	0	2
13	2010	Solomon Islands	5	3	2	2	0	3
14	2010	Cook Islands	6	3	3	1	0	6
15	2010	Nauru	3	2	1	1	0	2
16	2011	Niue	1	1	0	0	0	1
17	2011	Samoa	2	1	1	0	0	2
		Totals	94	58	36	48	11	47

Source: Forum EOM reports.

References

Commonwealth and Pacific Islands Forum, *Report of the Commonwealth Secretary-General's and the Pacific Islands Forum Secretary-General's Representatives to the Nauru National Assembly Election, 24 October 2004*, Commonwealth Secretariat and Pacific Islands Forum document, 2004 (2004a)

Commonwealth and Pacific Islands Forum, *Report of the Commonwealth Secretary-General's and the Pacific Islands Forum Secretary-General's Representatives to the Vanuatu National Assembly Election, 6 July 2004*, Pacific Islands Forum Secretariat and Commonwealth Secretariat document, 2004 (2004b)

Commonwealth and Pacific Islands Forum, *Report of the Commonwealth and Pacific Islands Forum Expert Team, 16 June 2005, General Election for the Autonomous Bougainville Government May–June 2005*, Commonwealth Secretariat and Pacific Islands Forum Secretariat document, 2005

Commonwealth and Pacific Islands Forum, *Report of the Commonwealth-Pacific Islands Forum Election Assessment Team, Papua New Guinea National Election, June–August 2007*, Commonwealth Secretariat and Pacific Islands Forum Secretariat document, 2007

Pacific Islands Forum, *Biketawa Declaration*, Pacific Islands Forum Secretariat document, 2000

Pacific Islands Forum, *Report of the Pacific Islands Forum Observer Group: Solomon Islands General Elections, 5 December 2001*, Pacific Islands Forum Secretariat document, 2001

Pacific Islands Forum, *Republic of the Fiji Islands National Election, May 2006, Report of the Pacific Islands Forum Observer Team, 15 May 2006,* Pacific Islands Forum Secretariat document, 2006 (2006a)

Pacific Islands Forum, *Solomon Islands National Election, Report of the Pacific Islands Forum Observer Team, 5 April 2006*, Pacific Islands Forum Secretariat document, 2006 (2006b)

Pacific Islands Forum, *Report of the Pacific Islands Forum Election Observer Team to Nauru's 2007 General Election, 30 August 2007,* Pacific Islands Forum Secretariat document, 2007

Pacific Islands Forum, *Report of the Pacific Islands Forum, Election Monitoring Mission to Nauru, 1 May 2008*, Pacific Islands Forum Secretariat document, 2008 (2008a)

Pacific Islands Forum, *Report of the Pacific Islands Forum Election Observer Team to the Republic of the Marshall Islands' Nitijela* [Parliamentary] *Elections, 19 November 2007*, Pacific Islands Forum Secretariat document, 2008 (2008b)

Pacific Islands Forum, *Report of the Pacific Islands Forum Election Observer Mission to the April 2010 Nauru General Elections*, Pacific Islands Forum Secretariat document, 2010 (2010a)

Pacific Islands Forum, *Report of the Pacific Islands Forum Secretariat's Election Observer Team to the 2010 General Elections for the Solomon Islands*, Pacific Islands Forum Secretariat document, 2010 (2010b)

Pacific Islands Forum, *Report of the Pacific Islands Forum Secretariat's Election Observer Team to the 2010 Election for the Offices of the President and Members of the House of Representatives of the Autonomous Region of Bougainville*, Pacific Islands Forum Secretariat document, 2010 (2010c)

Pacific Islands Forum, *Pacific Islands Forum Secretariat Election Monitoring Study: 4 March 2011 General Elections, Samoa*, Pacific Islands Forum Secretariat document, 2011 (2011a)

Pacific Islands Forum, *Report of the Pacific Islands Forum Election Observer Mission to the November 17, 2010, Cook Islands General Election*, Pacific Islands Forum Secretariat document, 2011 (2011b)

Pacific Islands Forum, *Report of the Pacific Islands Forum Secretariat Election Observer Mission to the May 7, 2011, Niue General Election*, Pacific Islands Forum Secretariat document, 2011 (2011c)

Pacific Islands Forum, *Forum Communiqué: Thirty-First Pacific Islands Forum, Tarawa, Republic of Kiribati 27–30 October 2000*, Pacific Islands Forum Secretariat document, 2000

Pacific Islands Forum, *Forum Communiqué: Thirty-sixth Pacific Islands Forum, Papua New Guinea, 25–27 October 2005*, Pacific Islands Forum Secretariat document, 2009

Spillane, Shennia, 'The Pacific Plan, 2006–15: Legal Implications for Regionalism', in Kenneth Graham (ed.), *Models of Regional Governance for Pacific Sovereignty and the Future Architecture of Regionalism* (Christchurch, New Zealand: Canterbury University Press, 2008), pp. 72–82

United Nations Security Council, *Statement by the President of the Security Council*, UN document (S/1998/287), 15 June 2005

Notes

[1] Any views or opinions presented in this article are solely those of the author and do not necessarily represent those of any of his former or present employers.

[2] Domestic guidelines for election observers were issued specifically for the 2005 election in the Autonomous Region of Bougainville, *Election Observation Guidelines: First Bougainville General Election 2005*; and guidelines were prepared for the 2006 Fiji general elections, *Guidelines and Code of Conduct for International Election Observers*.

Conclusions

Conclusions

Raul Cordenillo and Andrew Ellis

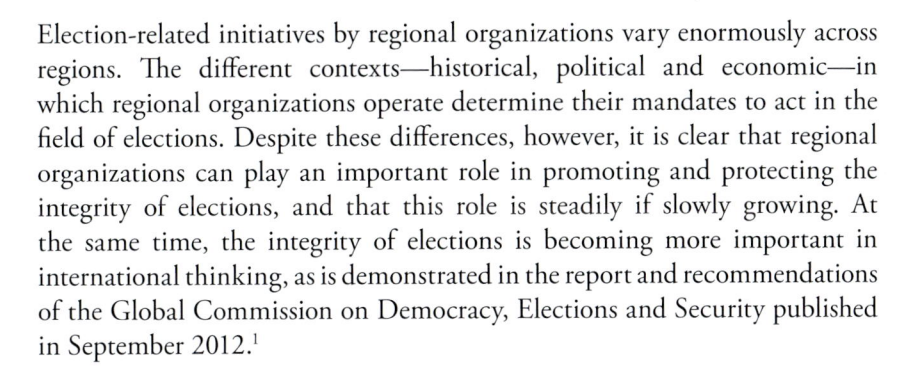

Election-related initiatives by regional organizations vary enormously across regions. The different contexts—historical, political and economic—in which regional organizations operate determine their mandates to act in the field of elections. Despite these differences, however, it is clear that regional organizations can play an important role in promoting and protecting the integrity of elections, and that this role is steadily if slowly growing. At the same time, the integrity of elections is becoming more important in international thinking, as is demonstrated in the report and recommendations of the Global Commission on Democracy, Elections and Security published in September 2012.[1]

While some regional organizations have clear guidelines on election observation and assistance (e.g. the African Union (AU), the European Union (EU), the Organization of American States (OAS), and the Pacific Islands Forum (PIF)), others do not and may yet have to seek a politically palatable mandate (e.g. the Association of South East Asian Nations, ASEAN, and the League of Arab States, LAS). While most organize or have organized election observation missions (EOMs), only a few undertake technical assistance or cooperation (e.g. the AU, the EU and the OAS). Some regional organizations seek to observe throughout the full electoral cycle, while others, often due to resource constraints, have not been able to achieve this. Although most electoral observation by regional organizations relates specifically to the electoral process, the PIF observation in Nauru is an example of a remit that covered more general issues related to the functioning of the political framework and process.

The chapters in this publication highlight the different experiences of regional organizations. While not exhaustive, they illustrate the innovations and challenges that each regional organization has faced or is facing in the field as they undertake EOMs, technical cooperation and gender mainstreaming.

At the Inter-Regional Workshop on Regional Organizations and the Integrity of Elections, the representatives of the regional organizations present stressed their regional peculiarities and differences in approach. At the same time, however, they acknowledged that they face common challenges and could learn from each other's approaches to addressing these.

Election observation missions

The majority of the chapters in this publication focus on EOMs by regional organizations—their history, purpose, methodology, institutional set-up, achievements and limitations. While pronounced similarities among regional organizations in this field are to be expected, given that a number have endorsed the Declaration of Principles on International Election Observation, there were notable, albeit sometimes subtle, differences:

1) All the regional organizations undertake election observation on request, except for the AU which requires its member states to invite in EOMs under the African Charter on Democracy, Elections and Governance. In addition, the 1990 Copenhagen Document of the Organization for Security and Co-operation in Europe (OSCE) institutionalizes a standing invitation to OSCE participating states to observe each other's elections.
2) The EU only undertakes election observation in third countries, because the OSCE undertakes observation within the EU by virtue of EU member states also being members of the OSCE. For the same reason, the OAS undertakes EOMs in all its member states except Canada and the United States.
3) The PIF undertakes election observation as an extension of the 'good offices' of its Secretary General.

The chapters highlight the fact that EOMs by regional organizations have variable levels of impact and they discuss several ways in which such EOMs could be made more effective.

1) The EOMs should abide by the Declaration of Principles and the Code of Conduct for Election Observers. The Declaration of Principles, among other things, helps organizations conducting EOMs to avoid falling into the trap of assessing elections as free and fair. Instead, the assessment is undertaken in line with the international standards to which states have voluntarily committed themselves.
2) The programming of EOMs should be informed by the electoral cycle. Deployment of EOMs should not take place only for election day, but should take on board developments during the pre-election and post-election periods.

Conclusions

3) In order to be effective, the implementation of recommendations put forward after an EOM should be followed up. Otherwise the same anomalies and irregularities are highly likely to show up again in future observation missions at future elections.
4) There is a need to further improve the methodology of EOMs, and to develop the capacity of observers and their wider understanding of electoral processes. Increased contact and interaction between regional organization EOMs and domestic observer organizations could form part of this process. To this end, exchanges of observation methodologies and experience among regional organizations, and between regional organizations and other EOM-conducting organizations, should be welcomed. Where consistent with mandates, this could extend to areas of wider importance to the integrity of elections, such as political finance and the independence of the media during elections.

Technical assistance or cooperation

Some chapters touched on the issue of the technical assistance or cooperation pursued by regional organizations. Initiatives in this area focus on improving the capacity of electoral management bodies (EMBs) to conduct elections. They range from the capacity-building training organized by the AU using the Building Resources in Democracy, Governance and Elections (BRIDGE) curriculum to the support provided for quality management systems (QMS) by the OAS.

The type of technical assistance or cooperation provided is really determined by the level of maturity of the EMB. OAS assistance to an EMB through a QMS, for example, will only be feasible if the EMB is familiar with its own processes and the services it provides to its clients. Nonetheless, the wider use of QMS may be put on the agenda for more general consideration by EMBs.

Moreover, technical assistance or cooperation becomes more effective if it is informed by EOM recommendations, and EMBs may find the recommendations made by regional peers and colleagues of particular relevance and value. In this way, technical assistance or cooperation takes on board the realities of the conduct of elections, and EOM recommendations are implemented in practice rather than merely being published and then gathering dust.

Gender mainstreaming

Gender mainstreaming requires more attention in the initiatives of regional organizations to promote and protect the integrity of elections. The OAS is the pioneer in this area through its development of a gender-sensitive election observation methodology. Next in line is the EU, which is committed to appointing a gender officer in each of its EOMs.

It is clear that ensuring the equal participation of women and men in electoral processes, as electoral participants, as electoral administrators and as electoral observers, remains a challenge. While it is not clear whether the structural innovations of the OAS and the EU, in particular, will help to address the issue, they certainly help put it on the political agenda and thus allow for dialogue to arrive at activities that could address unequal participation.

Domestic observation

Some EOMs, including some EOMs by regional organizations, link and cooperate with civil society observation initiatives. While there is no common thread that can be drawn from the differing regional contexts and mandates, contact and communication between EOMs and domestic observers can provide benefits, such as information sharing and increased understanding, for the EOMs, the host countries and the domestic observers.

Is there convergence?

When collecting the experiences of regional organizations in the field of elections, questions arise over whether there is convergence, where these points of convergence occur and whether they could form the basis for an international standard.

There is evidence of increased convergence among the regional organizations. This could perhaps be attributed to the Declaration of Principles and the annual meetings of the endorsing organizations, which serve as a natural catalyst. The Declaration could in the future become a universal standard for EOMs worldwide. Not all the regional organizations have endorsed the Declaration of Principles, however, and the different contexts and mandates of regional organizations will not make such endorsements easy.

Conclusions

Reflections

The role that regional organizations play in promoting and protecting the integrity of elections is growing by the day, as was shown recently by ASEAN's response to the limited invitation to observe in Myanmar. Mandates evolve and new initiatives come to life as member states reform. These changes in member states require regional organizations to take on new roles.

At the same time, there remains considerable room for improvement and innovation within the current initiatives of regional organizations, not only in the case of EOMs. In this context, there is value in learning from one another. Continued exchanges and dialogue among peers allow regional organizations to reflect on their actions and recognize lessons from other regional organizations that could be applicable to their day-to-day working and operations.

The Inter-Regional Dialogue on Democracy endeavours not only to facilitate such dialogue among peers but also to help regional organizations in their work on democracy building. This publication is one such opportunity for regional organizations to celebrate their achievements, and share them with their peers for their mutual benefit and increased understanding.

Notes

[1] Global Commission on Elections, Democracy and Security, *Report of the Global Commission on Elections, Democracy and Security* (Stockholm and Geneva: International IDEA and the Kofi Annan Foundation, 2012).

About the Authors

Julio Amador III is Foreign Affairs Research Specialist in the Center for International Relations and Strategic Studies (CIRSS) of the Foreign Service Institute of the Department of Foreign Affairs, the Philippines. He provides policy analysis and strategic advice to the Office of ASEAN Affairs, Office for Strategic Policy and Planning Coordination and Office of Asia-Pacific Affairs under the Department of Foreign Affairs. He has served as a member of Philippine delegations to ASEAN and other bilateral meetings and was recently supporting expert to the country's Eminent Representative to the Second East Asian Vision Group.

Franck Balme is the Domestic Observer and Regional Network Coordinator for the Network for Enhanced Electoral and Democratic Support (NEEDS) Project at International IDEA. He is an expert in election observation and electoral technical assistance.

Amor Boubakri is Legal Consultant for the United Nations Development Programme (UNDP) in Tunis. He was involved in the democratic transition process in Tunisia in 2011 as a legal expert for the High Commission of Political Reforms and Democratic Transition and he has been lecturing at the Tunisian universities on Constitutional Law and Human Rights since 1997.

Raul Cordenillo is the Head of the Inter-Regional Democracy Resource Centre, the Secretariat of the Inter-Regional Dialogue on Democracy and a virtual resource centre for democracy at the regional and inter-regional levels. Prior to this, he was Deputy to the Director of the International IDEA European Union (EU) Presidency/Global Consultations Project, Democracy in Development. Before joining International IDEA, he was Assistant Director at the Bureau for External Relations and Coordination of the ASEAN Secretariat.

Andrew Ellis is the Director for the Asia and Pacific Region at International IDEA, and previously served as Head of the IDEA Electoral Processes programme. He has wide experience as a technical advisor on electoral and institutional matters in democratic transitions. He acted as Senior Adviser for the National Democratic Institute (NDI) in Indonesia from 1999 to 2003, working with members of the Indonesian legislature dealing with constitutional amendment and reform of electoral and political laws, and with NGOs and political commentators; led the team responsible for European technical support to the Cambodian elections of 1998; and was Chief Technical Adviser for the Palestinian elections of 1996.

Pablo Gutiérrez was the Director of the Department of Electoral Cooperation and Observation at the OAS from August 2007 to July 2012. During his tenure as Director he supervised the deployment of 40 electoral observation missions in Latin America and the Caribbean and the implementation of more than 15 technical electoral cooperation projects. Prior to working at the OAS, Mr Gutiérrez served as Chief of Staff for the Ministry of the General Secretariat in the administration of Chilean President Ricardo Lagos Escobar.

Henry Ivarature is the Senior Programme Officer for the Asia and Pacific Region at International IDEA. Previously he worked as Regional Governance Adviser for the Pacific Islands Forum Secretariat and his positions held before that include those of Programme Manager of the Papua New Guinea Sustainable Development Programme; and Acting Director General and Papua New Guinea Senior Official to Asia Pacific Economic Cooperation (APEC). He also has ongoing interest in development issues in the Pacific Islands and has taught at the University of Papua New Guinea, at the Atenisi Institute in Tonga, and as a Senior Research Fellow at the National Research Institute in Papua New Guinea.

Shumbana Karume is the Head of the Democracy and Electoral Assistance Unit at the Department of Political Affairs of the African Union Commission. She has wide experience in the areas of electoral democracy, regional integration and other issues that cover governance and democracy in Africa. Prior to working for the African Union, she worked for the Electoral Institute for Sustainable Democracy in Africa (EISA) in South Africa, the Southern African Research and Documentation Centre (SARDC) in Zimbabwe and the United Nations.

Gillian McCormack is the Training Coordinator for the NEEDS Project at International IDEA. She has nearly 20 years of experience in training design and coordination and is a specialist in media frameworks for elections and media monitoring. She led 12 media monitoring missions for elections in the former Soviet Union for the European Institute for the Media and participated in four EU election observation missions as Media Expert.

María Teresa Mellenkamp is the Chief of the Electoral Technical Cooperation Section of the Department of Electoral Cooperation and Observation at the OAS.

Betilde Muñoz-Pogossian is the Director of the Department of Electoral Cooperation and Observation at the OAS. Previously she held the position of Chief of the Electoral Projects and Studies Section of the Department of Electoral Cooperation and Observation. She has worked on the development and systematization of electoral observation methodologies and has been an international observer and Deputy Chief of Mission in various OAS electoral observation missions. She has worked on democracy issues for the last 15 years.

Eleonora Mura is the Assistant Programme Officer for the Inter-Regional Democracy Resource Centre, the Secretariat of the Inter-Regional Dialogue on Democracy. Prior to working for International IDEA, she worked for the Roma Education Fund and the United Nations Mission for the Referendum in Western Sahara (MINURSO). Eleonora has a Master's degree in International and Public Affairs from the School of Government of the LUISS Guido Carli University in Rome and a Master's in International Relations from the University of Florence.

Domenico Tuccinardi is Project Director for the NEEDS project at International IDEA. He has extensive experience in managing electoral observation and electoral assistance programmes in several regions of the world. He was Delegated Commissioner for the Organization for Security and Co-operation in Europe (OSCE) in the first independent Electoral Commission of Bosnia and Special Advisor for the Independence Referendum Commission of Montenegro.